Love, Marriage, Divorce, and Remarriage:
A Biblical View

Second Edition

Love, Marriage, Divorce, and Remarriage:

A Biblical View

Second Edition

by Raymond E. Parry

RIDGEWOOD PUBLISHING

Published by Ridgewood Publishing
Woodland Park, CO

ISBN: 978-0-9889624-5-3

Cover design by Pegi Ballenger

Dedication

This book is dedicated to all those who have taught me about love and marriage: my professors, my wife Pegi, and my fellow travelers through life in the New Horizons class at First Presbyterian Church of Colorado Springs, CO.

Contents

Raymond E. Parry

INTRODUCTION

The understanding of love, marriage, divorce and remarriage among Christians has been unfortunately tainted by centuries of church misinterpretations of Biblical texts. Sometimes that happened in support of male-dominated traditions that perhaps deliberately overlooked the truly radical gender equality pronounced by both Jesus and Paul, and sometimes in support of limited doctrines of grace and forgiveness. Add to that mix nearly 100 years of romanticized notions of love, and we observe a divorce rate among Christians nearly the same as that among non-Christians in the USA, leading to confusion about the future value of an enduring marriage.

The following studies are my attempt to restore a thorough-going Biblical understanding that takes into account the first century social context as well as correct meanings of our received Greek text. I recommend having an open Bible handy while reading these chapters, or perhaps a parallel translation of several versions, or even a Greek-English interlinear New Testament if one is available. Incidental scripture references in this book are my own translation or paraphrase.

Study questions follow each chapter and can be used for individual reflection or for a small group study into what the Bible says about Love, Marriage, Divorce and Remarriage.

In preparation for this exegetical effort, I must acknowledge the teaching of my professors at Bethel Theological Seminary in St. Paul, particularly the late Robert A. Guelich, the receptive involvement of the New Horizons Adult Sunday School class at First Presbyterian Church over the last 20 years, and the effective cooperation of my wife, Pegi Ballenger, who listened with patience and dedication, offering constructive improvements to each chapter as they were written and presented in a variety of settings.

I hope these studies will help you, the reader, in your search for meaningful and supportive relationships.

1

BUILDING HEALTHY RELATIONSHIPS

You can't go through life without having relationships with other people of one kind or another: parents, brothers and sisters, spouse and children, friends, co-workers, fellow church-goers, and of course with God. In fact, the book of Genesis tells us we were created to be in relationship with God, which we messed up by trying to take control. Jesus set the foundation for our relationships by combining two Old Testament verses from Deuteronomy 6:5 and Leviticus 19:18. Read what Jesus said about the foundation for all our relationships in the Gospel of Matthew chapter 22:37-39.

37 Jesus said to him, "'You shall love the Lord your God with all your heart, with all your soul, and with all your mind.' 38 This is the first and great commandment. 39 A second likewise is this, 'You shall love your neighbor as yourself.' 40 The whole law and the prophets depend on these two commandments." (Matthew 22:37-39)

Jesus was answering a test question from a Pharisee about what is the greatest commandment, and he gave the man two answers, not just one. The first was love God with your entire being: your heart, your soul, and your mind; and the second one was love your neighbor as yourself. Ever since human life began on this earth, we have frequently confused those rules, and loved ourselves first, then those closest to us next, and God last, and ended up thinking life is all about ME. Or we may have put others first, then ourselves, and sometimes ended up in an unhealthy dependency relationship. Jesus' point was if we don't have God at the center of our lives, then our other relationships get messed up. We lose the central focus that brings the proper balance to all our other relationships. And if we don't love ourselves as God loves us, then we can't hope to love others effectively. We may instead use others to satisfy our needs that only God can satisfy. And if we turn those others into objects to be manipulated for our pleasure instead of seeing them as children of God like ourselves, then our relationships can become one-sided and hurtful.

There are some key qualities that all healthy relationships exhibit, for example, trust, forgiveness, and kindness. The Apostle Paul wrote about these qualities to the Christians at Corinth. We often read I Corinthians 13 at weddings, but that's not what he intended when he wrote that chapter. He was trying to teach the Corinthians what love really was, because they were confused about it after being immersed in a pagan culture.

Read what Paul said that love is, and isn't, in I Corinthians 13:4-8a.

> 4 *"Love is patient and is kind; love doesn't envy. Love doesn't brag, is not proud, 5 doesn't behave itself inappropriately, doesn't seek its own way, is not provoked, takes no account of evil; 6 doesn't rejoice in unrighteousness, but rejoices with the truth; 7 bears all things, believes all things, hopes all things, endures all things. 8 Love never fails." (I Corinthians 13:4-8a)*

Paul wrote this section on love as a corrective for the Corinthian church, which seemed to be a church filled with people who after their conversion ran around doing their own thing and not caring for others' feelings or well-being.

In the midst of their confusion, Paul said it was essential that the Corinthians understood that love is the most important characteristic of a Christian: Love for God, love for themselves, love for each other in the faith, and love for those outside the faith. In these verses from I Corinthians 13, we find that love is not just a warm fuzzy feeling for another, but a caring attitude that wants only the best for the other. Love is patient, love is kind, Paul says, and it celebrates the other's success or good fortune. Love is always truthful, always trusts, and always hopes. Love is the best side of us human beings. Love is not easy, because it requires us to deliberately decide to love, even when the other side of our humanness doesn't want to be patient, or kind, or truthful, or trusting.

Some Bible versions translate Paul's words in I Corinthians 13:7, as "Love always trusts," while the King James Version translates those same words as "Love believes all things." The word that Paul used means both to believe and to trust. In John 3:16, we find the same word is used for what we must do to have a healthy relationship with God. "For God so loved the world that He gave his only begotten Son, that whosoever believes in him shall not perish but have everlasting life." The last part of this verse could also be translated "whoever trusts in Him will not perish." So trusting someone else means that you believe they won't do you harm, but will do you good. You can safely make yourself vulnerable to someone you trust, and you know they won't hurt you.

Becoming a Christian helps you learn how to trust other people, because first you learn that you can trust God, and because second the Holy Spirit works in the lives of believers to help them become trustworthy. It takes two people to make a healthy relationship: on one side you have to learn to trust, and on the other, you have to learn how to be trustworthy. There's a difference between love and trust: To love someone else is a decision you make, no one has to earn it. Trust, on the other hand, is something that's earned, based on experience. To be considered trustworthy, you have to show yourself to be dependable. And if a person you trusted hurt you in some way, rebuilding that trust may take a long time. It also takes forgiveness.

Jesus taught his disciples in the Lord's prayer to ask God to "forgive us our sins, as we forgive those who sin against us." We need forgiveness because we sin against others as well as against God. And others sin against us when they violate our trust. It's part of human nature to think of ourselves and our own needs first, and that means others get hurt by what we do. So we need forgiveness because of what we do to them, and we also need to forgive what they've done to us. Forgiveness going both ways is essential in a healthy relationship.

Look at Colossians 3:12-14 to learn which traits the Apostle Paul said were essential to healthy relationships.

> *12 "Put on therefore, as God's chosen ones, holy and beloved, a heart of compassion, kindness, lowliness, humility, and perseverance; 13 bearing with one another, and forgiving each other, if any man has a complaint against any; even as Christ forgave you, so you also do. 14 Above all these things, walk in love, which is the bond of perfection." (Colossians 3:12-14)*

In the midst of verses that look a lot like what he wrote in I Corinthians 13, Paul said, "As the Lord has forgiven you, so you should forgive others." God's act of forgiving us for our sins comes when we accept Jesus Christ as our Savior. Because we are forgiven, we are then enabled by God's Holy

Spirit to forgive others who may have hurt us almost as deeply as we hurt God in the past. Without that power from God, we might find it too hard to forgive someone who hurt us badly. We can't do it in our own strength. Another quality that makes for good relationships is kindness. Note that in both I Corinthians 13 and Colossians 3, Paul said we should be kind.

According to my dictionary, being kind means to be gentle and compassionate and benevolent, which literally means "to show good will." The opposite of being kind is being cruel, to help clarify what being kind is not. Perhaps we've had past experiences when people were cruel to us, whether they intended it or not. And it hurt our relationship with them. Being trustworthy, forgiving and kind are key qualities that help build healthy relationships with other people, whether we are single, or whether we are married.

In I Corinthians chapter 7, Paul covered being single, getting married, becoming divorced, and the possibility of remarriage in detail because the Corinthians coming from a pagan culture were messed up in their relationships. Some Corinthian Christians appeared to be divorcing their non-believing spouses, so they could marry believers. Others were saying marriage was wrong, or that sex was wrong, and being single was more holy than being married. Paul let them know that being single was OK, being married was OK, and sex in marriage was OK. He did say it would be better for singles to stay single because they could then be more involved in ministry. He felt it was a gift of God to be single in this world, just as he was, because then you could focus on doing the Lord's work. If you were to marry, your focus would change to your spouse. Paul even says, "But those who marry will face many added struggles, and I want to spare you such problems." But, he went on, if singles want to get married that was OK, too. Paul summed up, it's not a sin to get married, and it's not somehow more holy to stay single. Living a Christian life and having good relationships is not a matter of being single or being married. It's a matter of following Jesus Christ and extending His love to the people you meet in this world.

Study Questions

1. How might you describe loving God with all your heart, soul, and mind?

2. What can we do when other people do things that make it difficult to love them?

3. What do you think Paul meant in I Corinthians 13:4 and Colossians 3:12 by being "kind?"

4. If a friend of yours was struggling in a relationship, what could you suggest to them that might help?

2

THE BASICS OF LOVE

I CORINTHIANS 13:13

As I was going through my divorce years ago, I had many occasions to think about the meaning of love. I had thought I knew what love was all about. It was simple. It was the attraction between two people that caused them to form a committed relationship that was supposed to last forever. When my wife left, I began to realize that my simple concept of love had a few holes in it. The cause and effect daisy chain had a few links missing. An automatic progression from attraction to love to committed relationship to forever did not compute anymore: love was not unconditional and marriage was not forever. I concluded that I didn't know what love was all about anymore, and that I also didn't know what marriage was either. It certainly wasn't what I had thought in my simple-minded manner.

After my divorce, I met a wonderful woman, and fell in love. I found I had to think about what was this deep hole called love that I had fallen into. How did these feelings come to be and what did they mean? How did I know it was love, and not something else? How did I keep from making the same simple assumptions about love that didn't hold water before? And marriage! What was marriage all about, I asked myself? How do two people form a successful union, and how does it stay together with all the pressures of modern life, and all the changes we ourselves go through, and the apparent ease these days of changing partners? I knew that if I was to have a healthy relationship with her and one that would form a healthy and long-lasting marriage, I had better figure out what love and marriage were all about.

So, what is love? First of all, love is a matter of the heart. Love involves your emotions. There is a chemistry that occurs between people in love that we can't explain. When you first met, it may have felt like some magic was at work. Feelings were being communicated and shared in a way that no one else could see or feel. The heart is what gives us the joy in being in each other's presence, of looking forward to the next step in the adventure of life together. Love is about feelings, the warmth we feel towards someone special in our lives, the chemistry that draws us to each other over which we seem to have no control. It is a physical, emotional, psychological attraction that draws people across a crowded room, just like the song from South Pacific says. There's goodness in that attraction. There's health for the relationship in the physical side of love, as we learn to give pleasure to the other instead of seeking it only for ourselves. And over the early years of our marriages, we see our relationship grow and mature and we enjoy being a part of each other's lives. Our joy in each other grows and blossoms, and hopefully spills out and brings joy to our families and friends. Love is a matter of the heart. And yet, as we all know, there may be days when we wake up and wonder where the magic has gone. The chemistry that seemed so vibrant and alive yesterday seems tired and worn out today. The heart will help us by reconstructing those early times when our love was so fresh and magical.

But love is also a matter of the mind. We choose to love another person. It's a matter of our wills: our willingness to give ourselves to another person, and our willingness to open ourselves to another and be vulnerable.

Like a Christmas present with a sticker on it that tells us when we can open it, there has to come a time when we say to our partner, "Open me please, I give myself to you." We have to give each other the right to our inmost thoughts and desires. But that gift of ourselves also includes our time, our energy, our listening attention, our holding and caring. Love is also a matter of our hopes, which exist in our minds. We hope for a life of safety, and a life of ease, and a life of constant companionship. And yet, as we all know, there may come days when those hopes seem to be dashed, perhaps by an unintentional hurt that comes from the one we love. And it's our will that makes us sit down and talk it through, when our heart wants to flee. It's our will that says, "I want to understand the source of my hurts, and how I've hurt you." And that force of will brings healing to both of us. That activity of the mind and will is also love.

But love first and foremost is a matter of faith. In 1 Corinthians 13:13, the Apostle Paul tells the Corinthians who may have exhibited tremendous faith but little love that of the three, faith, hope and love, the greatest is love. But I am of the opinion that love without faith will die.

13 "But now faith, hope, and love remain—these three. The greatest of these is love." (I Corinthians 13:13)

It will not survive the hard times that come to any marriage. In the book of Hebrews chapter 11, verse 1, it says that faith is the substance (or being absolutely sure) of things hoped for, the evidence of things not seen, which means that faith is the rock hard reality on which we can safely build our hopes and dreams.

1 "Now faith is assurance of things hoped for, proof of things not seen." (Hebrews 11:1)

Faith is not something weak, or something you turn to in the last resort. Faith is strong, and hopefully, faith was one of the strong attractions that brought the two of you together. Faith that God had brought you together, and wanted you to be together, will bring you through the tough times. There may well come times in any relationship or marriage when the heart stumbles in love, and when the mind no longer feels like choosing to love, and that's when a strong faith steps in to keep love strong. Faith that God is in the relationship and that God in His wisdom has brought two people together for His purposes as well as for our own. And that kind of faith can rekindle again and again the fires of our hearts and keep our marriages warm, and soothe whatever hurts have passed our way, and restore the precious hopes of our dreams.

A Christian marriage is built on love just like any other marriage. But it is built on more than just the warm feelings of the heart: it is built on more than just the choices of the will; a Christian marriage is built on a shared faith in the eternal God who loves each of us, wants the best for both of us, and wants us to share life together as a couple united for eternity.

STUDY QUESTIONS

1. If you are in a small group, share who was your first crush when you were a kid.

2. Which of the following songs (or another you might remember) best explains or characterizes your understanding of love when you were a teenager?
    I love you truly
    Let me go, let me go, lover
    Love is a many splendored thing
    Love me tender, love me true
    Portrait of my love
    Love makes the world go round
    Love, love, love, all we need is love
    Falling in love with love
    I want you, I need you, I love you
    When I fall in love
    People will say we're in love
    True love

3. From I Corinthians 13:4-7, list the 7 things "love is/does..." and the 8 things "love is/does not..." Which of each column is most important to you.

Love is/does...	Love is/does not...
1.	1.
2.	2.
3.	3.
4.	4.
5.	5.
6.	6.
7.	7.
	8.

4. Share one thing you love about your spouse or fiance.

5. If you had unlimited funds, what one present would you give your spouse or fiance for Christmas?

3

THE ORIGIN OF MARRIAGE

GENESIS 2:7, 18-24

One common problem often seen in troubled marriages is an overwhelming requirement by one spouse that the other spouse meet his or her needs. That's opposed to being able to meet one's own needs independently. The feeling of being needed may have been attractive in the beginning of the relationship, but over time it may begin to suffocate the other spouse until all he or she wants to do is escape. There are many examples in literature and the media where one person marries another to satisfy something they are lacking. Often the lack in these stories is security based, like money. The poor woman marries a wealthy man, or the gigolo marries the rich widow. Those may be broadly painted overstatements, but they reflect an underlying issue of getting our needs met that may affect our judgment when we decide who to marry, and who not to marry. I've heard comments that of course we marry out of some sense of needing the other person, or why else would we get married at all?

When I think about the needs we each have when we marry, I am reminded of the Garden of Eden story in Genesis 2. Verse 7 says "the Lord God formed man from the dust of the ground and breathed life into his nostrils, and man became a living being." We should take the time to draw a few conclusions from this verse: for example, being formed from the dust of the ground acknowledges that mankind is built of the same stuff our earth is made of, with the same chemical analysis, cell structures and atoms. That means we are compatible with our planet and our environment. We are not foreign bodies from some other world where ammonia is the atmosphere rather than containing the right proportion of oxygen we need. But we are not identical to our own physical planet, either, because humans have a unique mobility and adaptability that fall under the umbrella we call "life." There's a world of difference between a human being and a rock, which doesn't exhibit in any fashion what we'd call "life." Even a tree is different from a rock, and we might say it has life because a tree does have a beginning of its existence as well as an end. It grows from a seed into a tall and massive ordered arrangement of specialized cells, just like we do. It takes in sustenance and gives itself back to whence it came in a never-ending cycle. But that kind of life is not the same as the human kind of life, which includes an intentionality and ability to decide to change that a tree never has. A tree will never move by itself beyond its safe environment and decide to live where nature never intended it to live, as humans will. An animal has life too. It breathes, and forms relationships with other animals. Animals reproduce themselves in much the same way that humans do. Some animals, I understand, form life-long companionships, and even grieve when their partner dies. But, even though humans breathe and reproduce like animals, human life is different than animal life. Animals are content to leave things the way they are. It's not clear that any animal has ever had in mind the idea of changing the way the world is structured, or how groups of one kind relate to each other, as humans have done since the dawn of time. As Genesis says, there's something different about the kind of breath of life that humans have as opposed to animals. Genesis 2:19 reports that animals were formed out of the ground by God, too; but in verse 7, only humans are given

the breath of life that God gives to man. Read how the book
of Genesis depicts our human origins in chapter 2, verses 7
and 18-24.

*7 "Yahweh God formed man from the dust of the ground,
and breathed into his nostrils the breath of life; and
man became a living soul.*

*18 Yahweh God said, "It is not good for the man to be
alone. I will make him a helper comparable to him."
19 Out of the ground Yahweh God formed every animal
of the field, and every bird of the sky, and brought them
to the man to see what he would call them. Whatever the
man called every living creature became its name.
20 The man gave names to all livestock, and to the birds
of the sky, and to every animal of the field; but for man
there was not found a helper comparable to him.*

*21 Yahweh God caused the man to fall into a deep sleep.
As the man slept, he took one of his ribs, and closed up
the flesh in its place. 22 Yahweh God made a woman
from the rib which he had taken from the man, and
brought her to the man. 23 The man said, "This is now
bone of my bones, and flesh of my flesh. She will be
called 'woman,' because she was taken out of Man."
24 Therefore a man will leave his father and his mother,
and will join with his wife, and they will be one flesh.
25 The man and his wife were both naked, and they were
not ashamed." (Genesis 2:7, 18-24)*

But even the breath of life that God supplies which
makes man unique, doesn't make him complete. In verse 20,
it's reported that "for Adam, no helper suited to him was
found." Here in Eden all sorts of plants and animals lived as
God had created them, apparently with the ability to keep on
functioning the way plants and animals do, reproducing

themselves and continuing on for eternity in their pre-determined manner. Although nothing is specifically mentioned in this chapter of Genesis about there being both male and female cows and pigs and goats and chickens and lions and tigers and elephants, apparently that's the way God made them: male and female, with the ability to keep their species going forever. But note that Adam was created alone, by himself. A man without a mate. He may have all the facilities he needed for his part in reproduction, but the most important part — the woman's part — was missing. You might think it natural that God would then create the other half of the species, the part with the ability to have babies and keep the species going. But, if you said woman was created primarily for procreation, you'd be ignoring what the Bible says were God's reasons.

What motivated God to actually go and do the work of creating the female half of this human species was not the ability to reproduce, important as that is. In verse 18, God says, "It is not good for the man to be alone. I will make a helper suited for him." Adam has two needs that Eve can fulfill: he's alone, and he needs a helper. Companionship and completeness are two things Adam lacks. He has an emotional need for closeness that can't be totally filled by any number of cats and dogs. He has a need to communicate with someone who can communicate back, such as a person with whom he can speculate about the meaning of this life he enjoys, and hear back another viewpoint. But being alone also might suggest a lack of security that would be improved with another pair of eyes and another pair of hands and one more brain to process potential threatening conditions. And then there are things Adam just can't do well. God may have pronounced him good, but he didn't pronounce Adam perfect. There are things for which Adam's not qualified or he's not inclined to do, or he's not capable of. And for all those missing abilities, he needs Eve as companion and help-meet. "Help-meet" is the old English way of saying "helper suited for him." Helper, meaning someone who can fill in for his limitations.

The Rabbis used to say that at creation, Eve was taken from Adam's side leaving a gap, that can only be filled when Adam and Eve are united once again in marriage. Each one by themselves is an incomplete image of God. Only when bonded together do they become a complete picture of God in relationship within himself and with his creation. Men and women can't be totally complete by themselves without relationship. That's not to say that singleness can't be complete and satisfying, but that it takes a special gift from God to fill that emptiness and incompleteness that Adam felt in the Garden.

Do we have needs when we marry someone? Yes. The same needs Adam had for a companion and someone to make up for his inadequacies. Eve had the same needs, too, and Adam could be said to be a companion and help-meet for her as well. But, when getting your needs met overrides your God-given role of being companion and help-meet to your spouse, the marriage becomes unbalanced. An unhealthy co-dependency sets in rather than the inter-dependency God was after.

STUDY QUESTIONS

1. When we marry someone, what needs do you think there might be that we'd like them to meet that we can't meet on our own?

2. What might it mean to you to be alive because God breathed his breath into you?

3. What might the story of the creation of Adam and Eve tell us about God's relationship to us?

4. What are some ways you've found to keep the inter-dependency in your relationship balanced, so you are both satisfied and enhanced?

4

St. Paul's View of Love and Relationships

I Corinthians 7:1-7

St. Paul wrote more about love and marriage than anyone else in the Bible, and I Corinthians chapter 7 is almost entirely devoted to marriage issues. To understand why Paul wrote about love and marriage, we need to know something about the origins of the Corinthian church. The church at Corinth had only recently been formed, as we learn from reading Acts 18:1-4.

> *¹ "After these things Paul departed from Athens, and came to Corinth. ² He found a certain Jew named Aquila, a man of Pontus by race, who had recently come from Italy, with his wife Priscilla, because Claudius had commanded all the Jews to depart from Rome. He came to them, ³ and because he practiced the same trade, he lived with them and worked, for by trade they were tent makers. ⁴ He reasoned in the synagogue every Sabbath, and persuaded Jews and Greeks." (Acts 18:1-4)*

Paul first traveled to Corinth around 51 AD. To support himself, he joined some fellow tentmakers, Priscilla and Aquila, who had also just come to Corinth. They had been expelled from Rome along with all the other Jews by the Emperor Claudius and had moved to Corinth where they wouldn't be persecuted. At this time, Corinth was the fourth largest city in the Roman Empire. It had been destroyed in

146 BC by the Romans, then rebuilt by Julius Caesar, and resettled by retiring Roman soldiers who were given land there as payment for their service. Corinth was right on a narrow land bridge connecting Greece to the south with Macedonia to the north, so all traffic north and south went through Corinth. Many ships going east and west on the Mediterranean would also go through Corinth, because it was easier and safer to haul the boats over the narrow land bridge between the Aegean Sea and the Adriatic Sea than to go around all of Greece. Corinth was a city filled with soldiers, merchants, traders, and seamen; it was a city of commerce rather than culture. One of the high points of a visit to Corinth by traveling traders and seamen was the temple of Aphrodite, the goddess of love, which boasted 1000 temple prostitutes, through whom Aphrodite was worshipped. Imagine how difficult it must have been for Paul to preach the gospel to those traders and seamen, telling them about the one true God who isn't worshipped that way.

In addition to the difficulties of preaching the gospel in that environment, when you read Paul's letters to the church at Corinth, you discover that this church was filled with problems. One of the problems that Paul had to deal with in the young church in Corinth was that, while some of its members were converts from Judaism, most were Gentiles who had been raised in the Corinthian culture and shared its values. If it had been the other way around, with converted Jews being the majority, these problems may not have surfaced, because Jewish values would have prevailed. After all, what did love mean to these mostly Gentile Christians? Because of their background, love may have had more to do with the goddess Aphrodite and temple prostitutes, than an enduring and loving marriage that we find taught in the Bible.

The question of what was the meaning of marriage, and the place of sex in marriage was a hotly debated topic in Greek and Roman philosophies, and because of Corinth's location as a physical crossroad, it was also a philosophical and moral crossroad as well. For example, Gallio, the proconsul of Corinth mentioned in Acts 18:12, was the brother of Seneca the famous Stoic philosopher and tutor to Nero the Roman emperor. Seneca taught Nero honesty and love of virtue, which were important values in Stoic philosophy; but Nero turned out to be the most depraved emperor of all. Because of the interaction between the Corinthian "anything goes" attitude towards love and sex, and the Greek and Roman philosophies of the time, a wide variety of opinions could be found, not only in Corinthian society, but also in the Corinthian church.

Paul had left Corinth after 18 months of starting and nurturing the church there, but while staying in Ephesus in Turkey, he heard reports that there was flagrant sexual immorality going on in the Corinthian church, and members were winking at it. Some apparently held the position that it didn't matter what you did in the name of love. Look at what Paul said to the Christians in Corinth in I Corinthians 5:1-2.

¹ "It is actually reported that there is sexual immorality among you, and such sexual immorality as is not even named among the Gentiles, that one has his father's wife. ² You are arrogant, and didn't mourn instead, that he who had done this deed might be removed from among you." (I Corinthians 5:1-2)

Not only was this scandalous situation a violation of Jewish law, but also when Paul says that it was something Gentiles wouldn't do either, it may mean that the man's father was still alive and married to the woman with whom he was having the affair. The church should have responded to this blatant sin, but it didn't. There seemed to be no one taking responsibility for mentoring each other, or setting Biblical standards, and they were all going their own way.

To the other extreme, some people in the church were claiming that sex and marriage were evil and contaminated the body and soul. Sex, whether you are married or not, was bad for Christian holiness. Read I Corinthians 7:1 to see what some in Corinth said Christians should not do in their search to be holy.

> *¹ "Now concerning the things about which you wrote to me: it is good for a man not to touch a woman." (I Corinthians 7:1)*

Some Corinthian elders had apparently written a letter to Paul with a number of questions about how the Christian faith should be lived, and one question is found in the second half of verse 1. Paul himself is <u>not</u> saying "It is good not to be married," which is what some of the ascetics in Corinth would have said. Literally, the Greek says, "It is better for a man *not* to touch a woman." In Greek literature, "to touch a woman" meant to have sex. But this is not Paul's opinion, because he was not anti-sex, or anti-marriage. Instead, it was the opinion of some members of the Corinthian church who had brought their ascetic ways with them, and were trying to impose them on other members of the church.

Some scholars believe that Paul, as a rabbinical student of the famous Rabbi Gamaliel in Jerusalem had been married before his conversion to faith in Jesus the Messiah. To be a good Jew, says the Talmud, you should be married, particularly if you were a Rabbi. One list in the Talmud of those excommunicated from heaven began, "A Jew who has no wife, or who has a wife but no children." When Paul wrote this letter to Corinth, he was single, as we can read in verse

8, where he says, "To the unmarried and widows I say it is better for them to be as I am." Paul didn't set that as mandatory for all people, thank goodness, and we'll look at marriage in the next chapter. Anyway, it is very possible that after Paul professed faith in Christ, his wife divorced him for heresy. If that supposition is true, it might well have affected his views on marriage and divorce between believers and unbelievers, which we'll look at in chapter 10, St. Paul's Position on Divorce.

Paul responded to the assertion of some of the Corinthians that it was "good for a man not to touch a woman," by emphasizing the value of sex within marriage. Read I Corinthians 7:2-7 to see Paul's response to the issue of sex in marriage.

> 2 *"But, because of sexual immoralities, let each man have his own wife, and let each woman have her own husband. 3 Let the husband give his wife the affection owed her, and likewise also the wife her husband. 4 The wife doesn't have authority over her own body, but the husband. Likewise also the husband doesn't have authority over his own body, but the wife. 5 Don't deprive one another, unless it is by consent for a season, that you may give yourselves to fasting and prayer, and may be together again, that Satan doesn't tempt you because of your lack of self-control. 6 But this I say by way of concession, not of commandment. 7 Yet I wish that all men were like me. However each man has his own gift from God, one of this kind, and another of that kind." (I Corinthians 7:2-7)*

Paul says, because there is so much immorality, each man should have his own wife, and each woman her own husband. Now, he is not saying that everyone should be married, because he makes that clear in verse 7, where he says he wishes everyone were like him, and by that he means single, but he doesn't stop there. He goes on to say that each person has his or her own gift from God. He had received the gift of single-hood; others hadn't. That's an important point about being single. Being single is not merely your state of existence until you finally get your act together and find someone to marry. Being single for your whole life takes special grace from God; it's a spiritual gift, given so you as a single person can focus on ministry to God's people.

Paul came from a strong Jewish background, which taught that a man is not complete without a woman, going all the way back to Adam and Eve in the garden, where God said that Adam needed a helper fit for him, which actually means to complete what he was missing. Jewish thought saw men and women as two pieces of a jigsaw puzzle that were incomplete until put together. A man or woman by themselves didn't have all the skills, the wisdom, or the strength to face the challenges of life. Unless you have been given the special gift from God of singleness that Paul talks about in verse 7, life takes two working together as a unit to be successful. And this success depends on you recognizing the skills, strength and intelligence of your partner that he or she brings to the marriage.

Back in verse 2, where Paul says each man should have his own wife, and each woman a husband, he's not talking about every single person running out and getting married. He's saying that because of the rampant immorality in Corinth, every married man should be having sex with his own wife, and not someone else; and the same holds true for every married woman. He's talking about faithfulness and the loving expression of sex in marriage. He goes on in verse 3 to say that having sex with your spouse is more than just pleasure for yourself; it's an obligation you owe to your spouse. One of the purposes of sex is giving pleasure to the other. It's part of marriage, and it's something you shouldn't deprive your partner of. In verse 4, Paul says that our body does not belong to us alone, but also to our spouses, once we have become joined in marriage. Sex is not an expression of power of the strong over the weak, because the ownership of sex in marriage is joint ownership. Thus, this obligation is not something that can be demanded by one partner from another, but is something that can only be mutually given and shared.

In verse 5, he gives one exception to his rule that sex is a normal part of marriage: that is, if you both agree to not have sex for a short time so that you can devote yourself to prayer and not be distracted by other issues of daily life. But then Paul says, don't abstain from sex for a long period of time, because Satan may use it for temptation. Frankly, Paul says, you Corinthians are weak when it comes to temptation; you lack self-control. In verse 6, he says he's not commanding them to practice this exception, but only gave it as a concession.

To summarize this part of Paul's teaching on love and marriage, we conclude that Paul saw single-hood as a special gift. He saw marriage between a man and a woman as a relationship based on love and equality. He disagreed with the Corinthian statement about it being good for a man not to have sex with a woman, because it could lead to immorality among those with a lack of self-control. Instead, he recommended that married people see each other as having equal rights and obligations regarding sex in marriage. This position was quite unusual for his time, where male dominance was the norm. This was just as radical as what Paul said in Galatians 3:28, where he wrote that "there is neither Jew nor Greek, slave nor free, male or female: for you are all one in Christ Jesus."

In spite of the many people who have represented Paul as being a male chauvinist because of some of the other things he wrote, I think it's clear that for his time he was very much an egalitarian. He believed every Christian stands equal before God without regard to gender, nationality, or economic and social status. And he also saw marriage as a loving, caring, and sexual relationship, where each partner has an equal obligation to the other. As we study the rest of chapter 7, we must keep Paul's attitude of equality of the sexes in mind, because in almost every sentence, what he applies to men, he immediately follows with an identical application to women.

STUDY QUESTIONS

1. What have you heard people say about St. Paul's attitude towards sex or marriage?

2. What have you found to be some of the good aspects of being married or in a committed relationship?

3. What reasons do we have today to encourage marriage as opposed to just living together?

4. If Paul were here today, what do you think he'd say about our culture's attitude toward sex and marriage?

5

ST. PAUL'S OPINION ABOUT MARRIAGE

I CORINTHIANS 7:32-38

Being single vs. being married was one of the hotly debated topics in the Corinthian church. Paul wrote I Corinthians around the year 54 AD, only three years after the church had started. The reason for the letter was that some people in the church had developed extreme positions about what the Christian life should be like, and were trying to force it on others in the congregation. Apparently, these competing members of the congregation had imperfectly remembered what Paul had taught them, because his words were filtered through ears trained by the Corinthian culture. If you remember, Corinth was a large trading center, filled with merchants and seamen. One of its main tourist sights was the temple of Aphrodite, the goddess of love. On the other hand, one of the strong movements of Greek philosophy was asceticism, where purity and holiness came from denial of the flesh. In chapter 7:1, we read that some in the church were saying that it was good for a man not to touch a woman, or not to marry. Asceticism had become a part of the church at Corinth. Perhaps they saw Paul as a model of the perfect Christian, active in ministry, but single, and were now teaching that the only way to live a Christian life was to be single and devote oneself to the Lord's work, like Paul. Paul wrote this chapter to correct their understanding and expectations of single-hood, marriage, divorce, and remarriage.

Everything Paul says here must be looked at through the eyes and ears of a Corinthian, or you'll miss the force of what he says, and perhaps misunderstand his message. In the previous chapter, we talked about verses 1-7. In those verses Paul makes a strong case for marriage as a bulwark against the immorality of Corinthian society, for equality of husband and wife in marriage, and the importance of sex in marriage. He was arguing against asceticism, which said, "It's better to not be married, it's better to stay away from sex, and if you are married, you should avoid sex because it makes you impure." Jump down to verses 32-38 and see what else Paul has to say against this ascetic movement from another standpoint, and to look at some of the aspects of Christian marriage. Some of these verses sound odd from a modern standpoint, but we'll look closely at what Paul was really saying to singles who are thinking of marriage. Read Paul's advice to singles in I Corinthians 7:32-38.

> 32 "But I desire to have you to be free from cares. He who is unmarried is concerned for the things of the Lord, how he may please the Lord; 33 but he who is married is concerned about the things of the world, how he may please his wife. 34 There is also a difference between a wife and a virgin. The unmarried woman cares about the things of the Lord, that she may be holy both in body and in spirit. But she who is married cares about the things of the world—how she may please her husband. 35 This I say for your own profit; not that I may ensnare you, but for that which is appropriate, and that you may attend to the Lord without distraction. 36 But if any man thinks that he is behaving inappropriately toward his virgin, if she is past the flower of her age, and if need so requires, let him do what he desires. He doesn't sin. Let them marry. 37 But he who stands steadfast in his heart, having no urgency,

but has power over his own will, and has determined in his own heart to keep his own virgin, does well. ³⁸ So then both he who gives his own virgin in marriage does well, and he who doesn't give her in marriage does better." (I Corinthians 7:32-38)

Verse 32 starts out, "I want you to be free from any concern or care." The word translated *concern* or *care* is the same word Jesus used when he said in Matthew 6:25, "Don't *worry* about your life, or what you might eat or drink," Paul was being very pastoral and saying to the Corinthians, "I want you to be free from anxiety." What were they anxious about? What was causing them so much distress that Paul had to tell them not to be so up tight, so full of worry and cares? Paul goes on to say that an unmarried man can focus on, or be concerned about, the things of the Lord and how he can please the Lord, while a married man is concerned, not only about the things of the Lord, but also the things of the world, and how he can please his wife. The married man has divided loyalties, trying to satisfy both his wife and God. Paul goes on to say that the same thing is true about women. An unmarried woman can focus on, or be concerned about, the things of the Lord and how she can devote herself totally to the Lord. But a married woman's loyalties are divided, because she is concerned about pleasing the Lord plus the worries of this world and how she can please her husband. The bottom line is that as married people we spend a lot of time worrying about making our way in the world and supporting our families. Sometimes our time devoted to ministering to the world in the Lord's name gets shortchanged.

Note that Paul in these verses says both unmarried men and women and married men and women have concerns. Everyone is all anxious and worried, and that's what Paul told them not to be, just as Jesus instructed his disciples. All these worriers want to know how do you juggle your devotion to the Lord, and your relationships, whether you are married or unmarried. Apparently, the ascetic party in Corinth was telling people that it was better to be single, so that you could focus on doing the Lord's work, perhaps recalling something Paul had said when he was there. To them there was something more holy and more spiritual about being single, and not having divided and conflicting loyalties to satisfy. I think their ideas about the glories of being single were somewhat naive, because how many single people do you know who can focus totally on the Lord and not think about the other sex? It takes a special gift from God to be celibate, and most of us don't have it. If we were being forced by church authorities to live celibate lives, we'd have plenty of concerns, because celibacy doesn't come naturally.

Paul doesn't have any dispute with singleness, *per se.* He was single, and he found it easier to live life as a single, as we read in verse 28, where he says those who marry will face many added struggles, and he wants to spare them such problems, and again in verse 38, where he says that a man who marries a virgin does right, and the one who does not marry does even better. But he has an issue with forcing anyone to live one way or another. In verse 35, he says he's saying this for their own good, not to restrict them. In fact the Greek says he's "not putting a noose around their necks." He's more concerned that they live decent lives, because that's what "live in a right way" means. The word "undivided" at the end of verse 35 literally means without having anything drawn around you; in other words, unrestricted, with no noose around their necks. Verse 35 might be better translated this way: "I say this for your own advantage, not to put any restriction on you, but for decency and unrestricted devotion to the Lord." I think Paul is saying he will not place on Christians the requirement to stay single, like some in Corinth wanted them to do, because being single doesn't keep you from being anxious. There's nothing special about single-hood to make life go easier and smoother, unless you've been gifted by God as Paul himself had.

At the end of verse 37, Paul adds an issue related to relationships, one of decency. The decency issue he covers in verses 36-38, where he discusses the case of a man and a woman who are engaged to be married, and someone thinks this man is acting improperly towards his intended. Perhaps some of the church authorities are saying he should break off the engagement and stay single, because in some way that's more holy. Paul counters this argument by saying that the man needs to judge his own heart and whether he is gifted to celibacy, or not. Some translations report verse 36 saying some form of, "If she is past the flowering of youth." This is an unflattering translation for the three short Greek words that make up the phrase. Literally, the Greek says, "If is *huperakmos*" The word *huperakmos* is found only once in the Bible, right here in this letter to Corinth, so to understand it, we have to look closely at the word itself. It's made up of two smaller Greek words, *huper*, meaning over; and *akmos*, meaning the peak or highest point, just like our word "acme." So this phrase in verse 36 could mean "over the hill" or "past one's prime," although it's still not clear who or what is over the hill, the man, the woman, or the relationship. But, if we look outside the Bible to contemporary secular Greek literature, we find uses of *huperakmos* that have the meaning "the heights of passion." This leads one commentator to translate this word as "over-sexed." So some translations report this phrase as "if his passions are strong," and I think they are right. I don't think Paul was talking about a woman being so old that the man should marry her for the sake of decency, or that he was so over the hill that they should get married, either. It just doesn't make sense. Paul was probably saying that if the man feels overly passionate and can't restrain himself much longer from having sex with his betrothed, signifying that he is not gifted for celibacy, that he should go ahead and marry her. Paul is emphatic; the man is not sinning to marry his fiancee. They should get married. On the other hand, if the man searches his heart and finds that he has control over his sexuality, and is gifted to remain celibate, then and only then, he should break off the engagement and not get married. In both cases, as Paul says in verse 38, he is doing the right thing. What's important to Paul here is doing what's right and decent. Marrying or staying single does not determine whether you are living a Christian life. Instead, living the Christian life means treating people with respect and decency and being devoted to God.

In Jewish thought, a man was not complete without a wife, and that brings up the issue of personal wholeness, and whether we can be whole as a single person. I believe wholeness has to do with being healed and being in touch with God in your life. Thus, I think you need to become healed and whole as a single before you can form a healthy and whole marriage. Moving hastily into another marriage soon after a divorce is often a disaster because you are not healed from the wounds of the past, and you have not moved very far along the path toward wholeness before God. Paul said in verse 7, "But each has his own gift from God, one this gift, another that gift." In the context of this whole chapter, Paul was referring to his own gift of singleness, but also to the gift of being married. If God brought the two of you together, and you felt drawn irresistibly toward your spouse-to-be, then you have been gifted for marriage rather than single-hood. Because marriage is a gift of God, there's an eternal significance to it raising its importance far beyond most other earthly matters. When we struggle with what we think are important decisions in life, such as where we live, or what one of us does for a living, we need to remember that our marriage has eternal significance that is far more important than either of those issues. God gives us each other for his purposes, as well as for our own benefit. He knows that we need each other as part of his plan to help us mature into the kind of people he wants us to be: Christians who live and breathe a life of faith. And that's why Paul would say in marriage we are gifts to each other from God just as singleness for himself was a gift from God.

STUDY QUESTIONS

1. When you were a teenager, what did you think marriage might be like?

2. What do you think of Paul's claim that pleasing your spouse gets in the way of pleasing the Lord?

3. What anxieties have changed for you since you've been married or in a committed relationship from when you were single?

4. If one of your children said they didn't want to get married because of what they'd seen happen in your life, what might you say to them?

5. In what ways could you see your spouse as a gift from God?

6

St. Paul's Vision For Mutual Submission

Ephesians 5:15-33

In this chapter, we're going to look at a commonly misinterpreted section of Paul's letter to the church at Ephesus. Many people incorrectly use a part of verse 5:22 which starts, "Wives, submit yourselves to your husbands," as if it's the sum total of Paul's teaching on marriage. Well, you really can't interpret the meaning of that verse and apply it correctly unless you know the whole story, including what's written in the verses on either side of verse 22, and in other related passages in the Bible. Otherwise, you could end up supporting a male dominance that leads to wife abuse, or a "barefoot and pregnant" role for women, which the Bible itself does not support. Some have quoted Proverbs 31 as further support for the idea that wives should get up before dawn to make breakfast for their husbands, but Proverbs 31 doesn't really teach that. In fact, the reason that the good wife presented in Proverbs 31 gets up before dawn is that she is a land owner, a farmer, a trader, a craftsperson and merchant, and she has a busy day ahead of her. Gender roles may have changed since our grandparents' time, but God's plan for marriage was intended to have more equality and mutuality about it from the very beginning. So now, let's read what Paul really said about roles in marriage in Ephesians 5:15-33 and why he said it.

¹⁵ *"Therefore watch carefully how you walk, not as unwise, but as wise; ¹⁶ redeeming the time, because the days are evil. ¹⁷ Therefore don't be foolish, but understand what the will of the Lord is. ¹⁸ Don't be drunken with wine, in which is dissipation, but be filled with the Spirit, ¹⁹ speaking to one another in psalms, hymns, and spiritual songs; singing, and making melody in your heart to the Lord; ²⁰ giving thanks always concerning all things in the name of our Lord Jesus Christ, to God, even the Father; ²¹ subjecting yourselves to one another in the fear of Christ.*

²² *Wives, be subject to your own husbands, as to the Lord. ²³ For the husband is the head of the wife, as Christ also is the head of the assembly, being himself the savior of the body. ²⁴ But as the assembly is subject to Christ, so let the wives also be to their own husbands in everything.*

²⁵ *Husbands, love your wives, even as Christ also loved the assembly, and gave himself up for it; ²⁶ that he might sanctify it, having cleansed it by the washing of water with the word, ²⁷ that he might present the assembly to himself gloriously, not having spot or wrinkle or any such thing; but that it should be holy and without defect. ²⁸ Even so husbands also ought to love their own wives as their own bodies. He who loves his own wife loves himself. ²⁹ For no man ever hated his own flesh; but nourishes and cherishes it, even as the Lord also does the assembly; ³⁰ because we are members of his body, of his flesh and bones. ³¹ "For this cause a man will leave his father and mother, and will be joined to his wife. The two will become one flesh." ³² This mystery is great, but I speak concerning Christ and of the assembly. ³³ Nevertheless each of you must also love*

his own wife even as himself; and let the wife see that she respects her husband." (Ephesians 5:15-33)

Verse 15 sets the stage for what follows in Chapter 5. Paul is going to be talking about "how we live," and he wants us to live wisely in a world that is not only unwise, but often evil. He wants us to understand God's will for our lives, and not live foolishly and waste the opportunities God gives us. That summary of verses 15-17 is like the key point of a speech or sermon, giving you what the speaker wants you to remember if you remember nothing else. In verse 18, Paul contrasts those who fritter away the precious resource of their lives by getting drunk, with those who live life to the fullest by being filled with God's spirit. He wants us to sign up for the latter — being filled with God's spirit, rather than becoming saturated with the distractions of the world.

In verses 19-21, Paul lists four results in a Christian's life from being filled with God's spirit: speaking to each other in psalms, hymns, and songs; making music in your heart to the Lord, giving thanks to God for everything, and being submissive to each other. Many translations give us these results not as participles as they are in Greek, indicating something you are doing, but as imperatives, indicating something you must do, as if doing them leads to being filled with the spirit. But I think the sense in the Greek is the other way around — that these activities are the results of being filled with God's spirit, and not prerequisites. In other words, praising God for his blessings comes as a result of the spirit in your heart and life. It's what you do because of God's goodness in saving you, healing you, and making you whole.

The same is true of submissiveness; it flows out of God's spirit in your life. The opposite of submissiveness is trying to be in control. Many of us try to control every detail, and every aspect of our lives. Taken to an extreme, control can make us unpleasant to be around because we're cranky and negative. Psychologists say that trying to be in control can make us sick. In fact, the first step to healing in the 12-step program is to admit you're not in control, because trying to control life through self-destructive means is seen as the root of the problem. If we are filled with God's spirit, then we know that God's in control, and we don't have to be. We don't need to grasp for power. We don't need to take charge and have all aspects of our lives set and determined. We don't need all the people in our lives doing what we want them to do for us, so that we feel safe and secure. If we are filled with God's spirit, we can choose to be number two instead of number one; we can submit ourselves to other people who are also filled with God's spirit.

The submission that Paul talks about in Ephesians 5 isn't the normal everyday kind of submission to bosses, policemen, judges, and the like. Paul's talking about a Christian setting here where faith in God is a prerequisite. He's talking about a mutual submission, not a one-sided relationship where one person or group submits to some stronger person or group. Paul's talking about achieving the best for all concerned by giving up our right to be in control of the situation. We can only do that through God's spirit; it's a decision of our will to trust that God is in charge. When we let God determine the direction of our lives, the best results will occur. So, if you submit control of your life to someone else without a mutual faith in God, then there may be an underlying fear of what the other person might do to you, resulting in bitterness when you are taken advantage of.

In interpreting this passage, we have to remember that Paul is a preacher. I'm constantly amazed when I examine the structure of Paul's letters, at how many public speaking techniques he uses. You can't see it in the way the text is printed here for us, but when he lists four things that are the result of the spirit acting in our lives, it's as if he's ticking them off on his fingers, one, two, three, and four, to support his message of being filled with the spirit. And when he gets to the fourth point of mutual submission, he feels it's time for an illustration — a practical example of what it means to be mutually submissive. He chooses an area of life that he thinks the Ephesians need to hear about — marriage. The Ephesians didn't know what it meant to be mutually submissive in a marriage, let alone that marriage was intended to be a lifetime commitment.

The sanctity of marriage was unheard of in Roman and Greek cultures. Many of the Roman historians of the time remark about how frequently people were getting divorced and remarried. Juvenal, a Roman writer, reports of one woman who had had 8 husbands in five years. Jerome tells about a man whose 21st wife had been married to 22 men before him. The Ephesians didn't know what a Christian marriage should be like, so Paul uses this opportunity when he's talking about being filled with the spirit to tell them what an ideal, spirit-filled, Christian marriage would be like. He's presenting an ideal for the best of circumstances to people whose ideas about marriage were formed in the worst of environments.

In a Christian marriage, husbands are to love their wives as Christ loved the church, Paul says in verse 25. Paul's not talking about church buildings or church denominations here. He's talking about all the Christians that make up the church, he's talking about individuals whom God is saving, he's talking about you and me. How did Christ love you and me? He gave himself up for our sakes. He died that we might have life. It's an ultimate kind of giving. If we husbands give ourselves in that way to our wives, then we are submitting ourselves to their well-being. Submission means that our wives are more important to us than getting our own way or satisfying our own desires. Submission is an act of the will that raises up the other in our priorities, rather than lowering ourselves.

Paul says in verse 28 to love our wives as much as we love our own bodies. At one level, I think he's saying that whatever we decide to do should be as much value to our wives as it is to ourselves. Paul draws a parallel between Christ and the church, and husbands and their wives, using the analogy of a head attached to a body. To me, one of the most significant conclusions of his illustration is that you can't have one without the other. A head can't survive without the body, and the body can't survive without the head. The head may make decisions, but those decisions have to be good for the whole body. If we husbands love our spouses in submission to their needs, we will help them grow into the holy and blameless people God wants them to be, just as Christ loves the church and works to make it holy and blameless, as Paul says in verse 27.

If the submissive love that perfect husbands practice makes sure the ultimate needs of their wives are being met, the response of perfect wives is found in verses 22-24. As husbands show that they are filled with God's spirit, spirit-filled wives in a Christ-based marriage should be able to trust their husband's judgment, and submit themselves to their husband's leadership. But remember that submission is a result of being spirit-filled, not a prerequisite for it. You don't submit to another to become righteous in God's eyes. You only can submit yourself when you are so filled with the spirit that you can give up control because you know that God is in charge, not your spouse. This ideal picture of the perfect marriage suffers because we human beings are still self-centered. We haven't achieved the perfection God calls us to. We haven't totally let the spirit reshape our lives so that we really are spirit-filled. For imperfect and non-spirit-filled husbands to demand unquestioning submission from their wives is a violation of Paul's intent. There is no license for dictatorship or abuse in Paul's teaching in Ephesians. You cannot command submission — you can only give it.

Well, you might ask, so why is the husband the leader, and not the wife? Times have changed after all. Back then most wives stayed home taking care of the kids, while the men did the physical labor. Now everybody's at work trying to earn enough to pay the bills. Why not put the wife in charge, or at least on equal footing? I suppose some sort of system could be worked out, but I think it's common that when there are two people involved, there are going to be differences of opinion. Sometimes the wife knows more about a topic and she should be the one making the decision. Sometimes the husband knows more about a topic and he should be the one making the decision. But there are times when a decision has to be made, and there's no clear answer, so one person has to call the final shot, and Paul would say in those cases, a spirit-filled husband has the responsibility from God.

Of course, responsibility is a two-edged sword, because there is also accountability, where God holds you accountable for the results. In the Garden of Eden, before the fall, Adam and Eve were essentially on an equal plane when it came to decision making, because God made all the decisions. God decided what was good and what was bad for the world, and for them. As long as Adam and Eve deferred all the decisions to God, life was paradise. The problem came when they decided to take that power away from God and put it into their own hands. That's when they ate the fruit of

the tree of the knowledge of good and evil, and sin began.
God's solution was to define roles: Eve would bear children,
Adam would work in the fields. Both would suffer the pain of
their labor. But God would hold Adam accountable for their
decisions and actions as the head of the family. The same
holds true for any modern family. If a husband and father
makes a decision that affects the entire family, than he must
make sure it is best for everyone in the family, not just for
himself. The goal should be to find a solution where everyone
wins.

To summarize Paul's teaching on submission in a
Christian marriage:

1. Submission is the result of being filled with the spirit,
not a precondition for being filled with the spirit.

2. Submission is mutual: we are to submit to one
another, which means give up control and getting our
own way.

3. Submission takes balance: the wife's submission in
trusting her husband is balanced by the husband's giving
himself for her as Christ gave himself to the church, in
other words, being willing to die for her benefit.

Study Questions

1. What are some ways in which the change in gender roles over the last 100 years has been good for us?

2. How do you think trusting God might help you make better decisions in marriage?

3. How would you imagine being filled with God's spirit yourself might affect your family?

4. How can a husband show his wife that he loves her?

5. How can a wife show her husband that she loves him?

7

CONFLICT IN MARRIAGE

AMOS 3:3

In the chapter on the Basics of Love, I said love didn't mean feelings. Love is based on will, committing yourself to be there for another person. Feelings may attract two people to each other, and those feelings may get them to the altar. But what happens in the moment you say those wedding vows? When you say those words, you have passed beyond feelings, you are making a commitment to the other person in the sight of God and all those witnesses. Feelings of love may lead to marriage, but it takes will-power to make that marriage strong and enduring. Look at Mark 10:6-8 to see what Jesus said marriage should be.

> *6 "But from the beginning of the creation, God made them male and female. 7 For this cause a man will leave his father and mother, and will join to his wife, 8 and the two will become one flesh, so that they are no longer two, but one flesh." (Mark 10:6-8)*

In this passage in Mark, Jesus is talking to the Pharisees about what marriage means, and he quotes from Genesis 2:24 when he says that "a man will leave his mother and father and be united to his wife, and the two will become one flesh." When I was a teen-ager, I couldn't read that verse without thinking of sex. It was obvious to me: you get married so you can have sex without guilt. That was actually a pretty surface understanding of it all. The writer of Genesis was implying a depth of relationship as we find out when we read Genesis 2:20b-25 to see how this marriage relationship came to be.

> *20b "...but for man there was not found a helper comparable to him. 21 Yahweh God caused the man to fall into a deep sleep. As the man slept, he took one of his ribs, and closed up the flesh in its place. 22 Yahweh God made a woman from the rib which he had taken from the man, and brought her to the man. 23 The man said, "This is now bone of my bones, and flesh of my flesh. She will be called 'woman,' because she was taken out of Man." 24 Therefore a man will leave his father and his mother, and will join with his wife, and they will be one flesh. 25 The man and his wife were both naked, and they were not ashamed." (Genesis 2:20b-25)*

In the story of the creation of Adam and Eve, Eve, or woman, was taken from man's side, or flesh, so that he lost something in the creation of Eve. He was incomplete. He was missing something. But so was she, having only a part of what was originally whole. But in verse 24, man and woman are reunited in marriage: they become one flesh again, in other words, they are put back together so they are complete once more. The word "flesh" isn't about sex, it's about being made whole again through the relationship of marriage. I think that's what Jesus was getting at in Mark 10:8, when he concluded that the couple is no longer two, but one.

There's another familiar verse that I remember learning in my teenage years, and it's Amos 3:3. It comes from a passage when Amos was preaching to the Israelites in the 8th century BC. Speaking for God, he reminded them that they had been specially chosen, but had turned away from him, and if they didn't change their ways, disasters would come. Amos asks them a series of common sense questions, starting with this one, Amos 3:3: "Do two walk together unless they are agreed?" The answer Amos expected was, "Of course not." If you were a merchant needing to take a precious cargo from Jericho to Jerusalem up the road that was often traveled by robbers, you probably would ask someone to walk with you who you could trust. You'd agree to walk together. Amos' point was that God and the people of Israel had an agreement to walk together in a life of faith and service, but Israel wasn't honoring her part of the bargain. Their relationship was in trouble.

You have to have some measure of agreement to walk together in marriage, too. There are some things you must agree about to have a healthy marriage, and there are some things that you don't have to agree about, or don't have to agree about at this time. For example, here are some differences that can be irritations or can lead to conflict if you don't do something about it: do you sleep with the window open or closed? Do you wash the dishes after every meal, or let them pile up in the sink until it's full? Do you get to the airport way ahead of departure time, or just as they're closing the gate? Do you save for a rainy day, or spend it while you've got it?

But there are some areas that I believe you must agree upon for a healthy marriage: what city you live in, whether you have children or not, and whether God is an active part of your life. If you can't agree, you will often find yourselves in conflict, and many times conflict in marriage comes because of unresolved issues from the past, rather than just what's going on in the present. Not only conflict from past relationships, but from childhood frustrations with your parents. Harville Hendrix wrote a book entitled "Getting the Love You Want," and in it, he said that we often marry someone that reminds us of our caregivers, even if it's subconscious. Some things we liked about our parents we see in our spouse, and that's one of the reasons we're attracted to them. However, there are also some things that our spouse does that remind us of things we didn't like about our parents, that bring up ancient angers, hurts and fears. We get hooked or flare up, because we never learned how to deal with them. Hendrix would say we often pick the spouse we marry because they feel very familiar to us, but subconsciously we hope they can help us work through those ancient pains. Consciously, we may not even see it that way. We may see just the irritating behavior, or the destructiveness of it, just like with Mom and Dad, and we behave in just the same way we did with them. We may get angry at our spouse just like we did with our parents, or fearful and disabled.

Wisdom comes when we realize that instead of anger or fear, we need to learn a healthy alternate behavior. It's as if God picked out our spouse specifically to give us another chance to finish the unfinished work of growing up, and conflicts are going to occur. One thing that happens when you're in conflict is fear: you're getting in touch with the feelings you had when you were a kid about some big scary adult. That's when a spouse needs to be extra kind and recognize that their spouse is down there in their little fearful kid self, and needs love and compassion.

A number of years ago, I picked up a book on conflict that I found very valuable called "Church Fights: Managing Conflict in the Local Church," by Speed Leas and Paul Kittlaus. I used the principles it taught to help a small group in the church I attended to resolve a conflict that was tearing it apart. While the book was aimed at conflicts in the church, the principles it taught applied to marriage as well. The first principle was that not all conflict is bad. Some conflict is actually good, because it forces you to deal with issues, and if you deal with the issues in a positive way, it strengthens the marriage. If we hang in there through the conflict, we can help each other grow. Conflict doesn't mean shouting and yelling. It means two people have different needs that can't be satisfied at the same time, or two people hold different values that cause them to frequently disagree about what to do next.

Absence of conflict may not be a sign of harmony, but of apathy — the people really don't care what happens — and apathy in a marriage is just as deadly as a destructive conflict. Destructive conflict happens when an irritation or difference in values escalates into put-downs, or name-calling, or isolation of the parties, or even violence. Deciding to not talk about an issue can actually be as harmful as fighting about it, because avoiding or repressing doesn't make the problem go away. It will resurface later. And sometimes, when each person shares their position, without interruption, you find there really wasn't a real difference after all, it just seemed that way.

Conflict is good only when the two people involved commit themselves to work to get it resolved. Working together on a project helps strengthen a marriage, and working on a conflict can be just like working together on a project like installing a sprinkler system, or building a house. First you have to decide if the conflict is too big to handle yourself. If it's already escalated to the "we can't talk about it" stage, you need a referee, someone else to help you talk about it safely. Or if too many emotions come out at anything that sounds related to the problem, so that you feel you're walking on egg-shells around the other person, you need a referee. Or if it's gotten so bad you're sleeping in separate rooms, or don't eat together, you need someone else to help moderate the conflict.

For many areas of conflict, you can follow a five step process that allows you to step back from the conflict, and deal with it objectively. You can take the emotion out of it and work together on a solution. First you have to agree to work on it. It doesn't do any good if only one of you wants to work on it — it takes both of you. Second, you've got to agree to let each other express themselves fully, without the other butting in, contradicting or defending themselves. Third, you've got to agree on the end goal. If you have a conflict over which family to visit during the holidays, a suitable goal might be to have both of you feel connected to your own family by the end of the holiday season. Once that's done, you know you have to work together to figure out a way to reach the goal. Fourth, you've got to agree that you are equally important, and that satisfying both your needs is important. Fifth, you've got to agree on a decision-making process, such as does one person make the final decision and the other go along with it, or do you does each person have the right to suggest solutions, and you're not done till both are satisfied.

If this sounds like work, it is. A good marriage takes work and effort, it doesn't come easily. If it sounds like too much work, find someone who can be objective to help you through the process. The key to making marriage successful is making it intentional, not accidental. A good marriage doesn't happen by accident. I think this principle underlies what Genesis 2:24 means when it says the man leaves his parents and is joined to the woman, and the two become one. That one verse contains three intentional statements: leaves, joins, becomes. It takes will, it takes work, and of course, it takes love.

STUDY QUESTIONS

1. If you are married, do you remember why you decided to get married, when you could have stayed single?

2. What do you think it means to be "one" when there's two of you?

3. What differences can happen between two people that often become irritations?

4. What areas in life do you think it's important for a couple to agree upon?

5. Have you found that you have instant reactions to something your spouse or partner says or does that belong somewhere in your past?

6. What kinds of conflicts do you think need the outside help of a counselor?

8

Giving Grace to Each Other

Colossians 3:12-15

When we grow up together as a family, it is inevitable that conflicts occur, and that someone is going to feel hurt. The Bible is full of stories of conflict in families. In God's lovely Garden of Eden, Adam blames Eve for both of their disobedience of God's plain instructions. Then Cain, their son, kills Abel out of jealousy. Generations later, Jacob acquires his twin brother Esau's birthright in a shrewd deal, but then stole his father Isaac's blessing, which should have gone to Esau, through outright deception. Many chapters of Genesis are spent on tracing Jacob's adventures, but only one chapter is devoted to Esau, and it's just a list of his descendants. The irony is that Esau, the brother we rarely honor, forgave his brother Jacob and welcomed him back with open arms, while Jacob, the brother we hear about most often, expected Esau to be resentful and revengeful, perhaps because that's how he'd have been if the roles were reversed.

In the Old Testament, the concept of sin and forgiveness focuses on the relationship between a person and God. A person rebels against God's authority in his or her life, thus sinning against God. When they admit their guilt and pledge to return to God's authority, then God forgives them, and as Psalm 32:2 says, he doesn't count it against them any more. But also in the Old Testament, no matter who you hurt, it's God you are really sinning against, and it's

God who is the final source of forgiveness. I think that's best illustrated by the story of Joseph and his brothers from the book of Genesis, Chapters 37-50, and how they sold him into slavery. If anyone could have harbored ill will toward his brothers, it would have to be Joseph. Sure enough, the tables were turned, and the brothers seek charity from Joseph in Egypt, where he's risen high in Pharaoh's court. And Joseph grants them food and a place to stay while the famine in Palestine continues. But after Jacob dies, Joseph's brothers are concerned that Joseph will take revenge against them for selling him into slavery years before, so they say to Joseph in Genesis 50:16-19, "our father wants you to forgive us for our sins against you." Joseph's response is interesting, because he essentially says, "Am I God?" In other words, Joseph is reiterating an Old Testament concept, that when you sin against someone, you are sinning against God, which is a greater sin, and only God can forgive you of that sin.

I think Joseph's response helps explain the reaction of the rabbis when Jesus healed the paralytic in Capernaum in Mark 2:1-12, the one who was lowered by ropes through the roof by his friends. If you remember, Jesus simply said to him in Mark 2:5, "Son, your sins are forgiven." The rabbis were upset, and they asked, "Who can forgive sins except God alone?" The rabbis taught that you should forgive people of sins they've committed against you, if they ask you to. They also taught that if someone asks you to forgive them, and you decline, then you become the guilty party, and God's anger turns from them to you, and you need to seek forgiveness for your sin of not being forgiving. But, there is nothing in the story of the paralytic to suggest he had hurt Jesus in any way, nor did he ask for forgiveness from Jesus, so there would have been no need for Jesus to forgive him. I'm sure that's how the rabbis sitting there, watching, saw the situation. But as Jesus explained, he forgave the paralytic his sins to show that he had God's authority behind him, and showed also that forgiveness of sins leads to changed and healed lives, as was dramatically demonstrated by the paralytic getting up and walking.

Jesus attempted to broaden the common concept of forgiveness, when he taught his disciples in the Lord's prayer (Matthew 6:12) to ask God to "forgive us our sins, as we forgive those who sin against us." Often that phrase is interpreted that if we forgive the sins of others, God will forgive us our sins. And, if we turn that upside down, and look at it negatively, as the Rabbis would have, we'd read instead, "if we don't forgive the sins of others, God will not forgive us our sins." As a graduate of the famed rabbinic school of Gamaliel, the Apostle Paul took a different look at that principle in Colossians 3:13, based on Christ already having died for our sins. Paul said, "Because God has forgiven our sins, we should forgive the sins of others." Rather than forgiving others so that we might be forgiven, God's act of forgiveness is already complete when we accept Jesus Christ as our Savior. Because we are forgiven, we are enabled by God's Holy Spirit to forgive others who may have hurt us as deeply as we hurt God in the past. Look at what Paul said about forgiveness in Colossians 3:12-15.

> [12] *"Put on therefore, as God's chosen ones, holy and beloved, a heart of compassion, kindness, lowliness, humility, and perseverance;* [13] *bearing with one another, and forgiving each other, if any man has a complaint against any; even as Christ forgave you, so you also do.*

> [14] *Above all these things, walk in love, which is the bond of perfection.* [15] *And let the peace of God rule in your hearts, to which also you were called in one body; and be thankful." (Colossians 3:12-15)*

Verses 12-14 are very practical instructions, in very simple language, telling us how we should behave toward each other in the church, in our jobs, and in our families. Because we are God's chosen people we should be changed in the way we behave towards each other. As Christians, we shouldn't reflect what we see on TV today, or read in the newspapers and magazines. There should be something different about those of us who have accepted Jesus Christ as Lord and Savior. There should be something different about the way we do our jobs. There should be something different about our families and our marriages. That doesn't mean we're not going to have problems, because neither we nor anyone else in our families are perfect. In spite of how we'd like to be, we will continue to hurt each other from time to time. Otherwise, Paul wouldn't be telling us to forgive each other.

We wouldn't need to be told to forgive others, except we're imperfect. Verse 13 begins with the phrase "bear with each other." Now the Greek word *anexomenoi* literally means to "hold up," so I prefer to translate it as "supporting" rather than "bear with." It's a participle implying continuous action, so Paul is encouraging us to support each other continually. Paul goes on to say in verse 13 that we should "forgive whatever grievances you may have against one another." The Greek word Paul uses for "forgive" is *charizomenoi*, which comes from *charis*, which means "grace." Because *charizomenoi* is also a participle implying continuous action, I would equate "forgiving" to "the act of giving grace." Now, what does it mean to give grace to each other? Grace means forgiveness, for one thing. Theologically, it refers to God's unmerited favor to us. We don't deserve it, he chooses to care for us in spite of what we've done. So grace also involves patience, and loving kindness, and wanting the best for us. Grace has become such a theological

word, we tend to think of it as something that only God
gives. But, Paul concludes verse 13 by saying literally, "as
indeed the Lord forgave (or gave grace to) you, so you also."
It's an elliptical sentence, finished by repeating the verb, "As
the Lord forgave you, so you forgive others." As the Lord
gave you grace, so you give grace to others. As Christians, we
are to follow the example of Jesus, who gave grace to the
paralytic and changed his life. We are to give grace, or
forgiveness, to others and change their lives.

While Jesus definitely supported the profound truths
and lessons of the Jewish faith, he radically clarified the
responsibilities of people of faith in God. He claimed we
would perform miracles greater than he did. He said we
would have the same authority to forgive sins as he did. In
the Sermon on the Mount, he presented a way of life that was
so different from the way the average life was lived, that it
could only be lived by people enabled by God's Holy Spirit.
He knew we'd never achieve perfection, or he wouldn't have
told us to say, "forgive us our sins," but he knew we could
grow toward perfection through trusting in God's power to
change our lives.

The family is a good place to practice "giving grace"
and "forgiveness." Marriage gives us plenty of opportunity to
extend forgiveness, because we have plenty of opportunity to
get into conflict and hurt each other. It's so hard to get those
words out, "I forgive you." And "please forgive me." But it's
so essential, because our marriage is our primary
relationship after our relationship to God. I've found that I
frequently need to remind myself that I need to forgive and
be a giver of grace in my marriage, so that we both can be
healed and be the kind of people God wants us to be. But I
also need to exhibit humility and seek forgiveness when I do
wrong. God gives us a partner because He knows our lives

and our ministries can be so enhanced if we're not trying to do it alone. But He also has given us forgiveness through Jesus Christ to show us how relationships can be restored. Our relationship with God was once broken, but now it can be good again through forgiveness. Our relationship with our spouse might be strained or troubled, but it too can be made good again through forgiveness. All it takes is to simply say, "I'm sorry, please forgive me."

Study Questions

1. What do you remember doing when you were a child that caused your parents concern?

2. How do you think a sin against someone else might be a sin against God?

3. If your life had been changed as dramatically as the paralytic's in Mark 2:1-12, what might you have thought about the power of forgiveness?

4. When you think about the future, what kinds of support do you think you might need?

5. How do you think your marriage or committed relationship might change if you practiced forgiveness on a daily basis?

9

JESUS' STORY ABOUT GOD'S FORGIVENESS

LUKE 15:11-24

One of the best stories in the Bible that illustrates forgiveness is Jesus' story of the Prodigal Son. The characters in this story that Jesus told seem so real that they could be our neighbors, or perhaps even ourselves. Many of us have been there: we've either been the son or daughter who takes leave of the safety of a relationship and goes out bravely into the world and makes a mess of it; or, we've been the anxious parent, worried sick about the absent son or daughter, whether they're safe, or eating right, or forming the right friendships, or spending their money wisely; or, we've been the older brother or sister that resents sharing the parents love and attention with the wild and unruly younger child who always seems to get their way, and for whom life seems to have no consequences. No matter which character we imagine ourselves to be, the story illustrates the power of forgiveness in rejuvenating relationships, and keeping them free of animosity and bitterness. Read Jesus' story in Luke 15:11-24 about God's forgiveness in the Parable of the Prodigal Son.

> *11 "He said, "A certain man had two sons. 12 The younger of them said to his father, 'Father, give me my share of your property.' He divided his livelihood between them. 13 Not many days after, the younger son gathered all of this together and traveled into a far country. There he*

wasted his property with riotous living. ¹⁴ When he had spent all of it, there arose a severe famine in that country, and he began to be in need. ¹⁵ He went and joined himself to one of the citizens of that country, and he sent him into his fields to feed pigs. ¹⁶ He wanted to fill his belly with the husks that the pigs ate, but no one gave him any. ¹⁷ But when he came to himself he said, 'How many hired servants of my father's have bread enough to spare, and I'm dying with hunger! ¹⁸ I will get up and go to my father, and will tell him, "Father, I have sinned against heaven, and in your sight. ¹⁹ I am no more worthy to be called your son. Make me as one of your hired servants."'

²⁰ "He arose, and came to his father. But while he was still far off, his father saw him, and was moved with compassion, and ran, and fell on his neck, and kissed him. ²¹ The son said to him, 'Father, I have sinned against heaven, and in your sight. I am no longer worthy to be called your son.'

²² "But the father said to his servants, 'Bring out the best robe, and put it on him. Put a ring on his hand, and shoes on his feet. ²³ Bring the fattened calf, kill it, and let's eat, and celebrate; ²⁴ for this, my son, was dead, and is alive again. He was lost, and is found.'" (Luke 15:11-24)

Jesus told this story as an example of our basic relationship to God. The father represents God who lets us make our own decisions, lets us go our own way, lets us make a mess of our lives if that's what we want to do; but then welcomes us back with open arms when we have become disenchanted with doing our thing and having our own way. This is a story about forgiveness—about God's forgiveness to his wayward people, about his forgiveness to us as individuals, when we, in spite of all our good intentions, hurt others, or were hurt by others, to the point of no return; and no amount of human forgiveness given or offered seems anywhere near enough to patch the awesome crack that tore our relationships apart. And yet, the good news of this story is that God offers his forgiveness to us not only freely and without strings attached, but more abundantly that our worst behaviors and sins could anticipate.

The Old Testament offers a similar drama about forgiveness in the story of the prophet Hosea and his wife Gomer. Hosea and Gomer lived in the 8th century before Christ in the northern part of Israel. Politically, the northern kingdom became strong under the leadership of King Omri and his son, Ahab, the one who married Jezebel. But religiously, they turned far away from God to worship the Baals and other idols of the nations around them. Hosea the prophet proclaimed a message of God's judgment on the Israelite people for their sins and their rejection of God, but he also proclaimed a message of God's forgiveness if they turned from their sins, and came back to him. And he did it through the example of his own marriage.

The prophets of Israel quite often acted out their message, to make the point very clear to people who didn't always want to hear a spoken message from God. As an enactment of God's relationship to the people, Hosea married Gomer, who apparently had been a cult prostitute for Baal worship, and they had three children. Hosea was portraying God, who had bound himself in covenant to the Israelites. They, however, constantly betrayed Him and worshipped other gods, a form of spiritual adultery. Gomer is disloyal to Hosea and runs away after other men.

Eventually, she sinks so low that she becomes a slave and at a slave auction, Hosea sees her and buys her back, and restores her to his family as wife and mother. The visual lesson for the people is that no matter how far they stray from God, God will forgive and take them back. God loved his people as human beings love and care for their children. Even when they reject him and go from him, he can't give them up. He has compassion on them and will take them back, even as Hosea took Gomer back. Look for the tender words in Hosea 11:8-9 which follow the words of disappointment Hosea spoke in God's name in verses 1-7 to the people of Israel.

> ¹ *"When Israel was a child, then I loved him,*
>   *and called my son out of Egypt.*
> ² *They called to them, so they went from them.*
>   *They sacrificed to the Baals,*
>   *and burned incense to engraved images.*
> ³ *Yet I taught Ephraim to walk.*
>   *I took them by his arms;*
>   *but they didn't know that I healed them.*
> ⁴ *I drew them with cords of a man, with ties of love;*
>   *and I was to them like those who lift up the yoke on*
>   *their necks;*
>   *and I bent down to him and I fed him.*
>
> ⁵ *"They won't return into the land of Egypt;*
>   *but the Assyrian will be their king,*
>   *because they refused to repent.*
> ⁶ *The sword will fall on their cities,*
>   *and will destroy the bars of their gates,*
>   *and will put an end to their plans.*
> ⁷ *My people are determined to turn from me.*
>   *Though they call to the Most High,*
>   *he certainly won't exalt them.*

⁸ "How can I give you up, Ephraim?
    How can I hand you over, Israel?
    How can I make you like Admah?
    How can I make you like Zeboiim?
My heart is turned within me,
    my compassion is aroused.
⁹ I will not execute the fierceness of my anger.
    I will not return to destroy Ephraim:
    for I am God, and not man; the Holy One among
        you;
    and I will not come in wrath." (Hosea 11:1-10)

Both Jesus' story of the Prodigal Son and the example
of Hosea and Gomer teach us that God forgives us. It is part
of God's nature to be forgiving. To be God means to forgive.
And to be like God means to be forgiving like God is. That is
part of our call as Christians. We are to spread the good news
that the kingdom of God has come on earth so that others
might have a personal relationship with God through Jesus
Christ. The Good News means that Jesus came and died to
save us from the just penalty for our sins, and we can be
forgiven. No matter how bad the world has become, no
matter how much people perpetrate evil, or how destructive
we are in our closest relationships, God will forgive those
who repent and return to Him. If we, instead of God, were in
charge of the world, we might be tempted to wipe it all out
and start over again. We might be tempted to consign
someone who hurts us to the deepest hell. But God doesn't
think like we do. He doesn't act like we do. Instead, God sent
his only son as a defenseless little baby as a sign of his
presence bringing forgiveness to our human lives. Because
God will forgive us of our deepest failings, we have the power
through God's Spirit to forgive each other for the hurts and

anguish of the past, and forgive ourselves for the hurts and anguish we've caused others.

Marriage is a good place to practice forgiving someone else, mirroring God's act of forgiving you. In marriage, two individuals come together from different backgrounds and experiences. Each of us has had our successes and our failures. For many of us, one of those failures was the failure of a marriage. No matter how that relationship was broken, no matter who filed for divorce, no matter who had an affair, there were enough human failings on both sides to challenge our ability to forgive. Even in a new relationship, where you don't want to repeat any of those mistakes of the past, because you are human, you may well hurt your partner from time to time, and you also may be hurt from time to time. It's part of the package. Someone has said, you can't love someone else without making yourself vulnerable to getting hurt.

I think many people hurt us when they are so caught up in their own lives, dealing with their own pain, that what they do to reduce their own inner turmoil injures us. None of these reasons for hurt are excuses, only attempts to explain where they come from. Bottom line, if you are in a relationship, you may get hurt from time to time, sometimes just a little bit, and sometimes a lot. And yet, if we dwell on the hurt, it will only damage us—it will never fix the hurt or change the one who hurt us. And that's where forgiveness comes in.

No matter how many times we hear about forgiveness, it seems we need to hear about it again and again. Forgiveness may be one of the hardest things we do for someone else, or to accept for ourselves. Forgiveness is a decision we make, whether it's to forgive someone else or to forgive ourselves. Forgiveness is not a feeling. If we sit and wait around for the feeling of being forgiven or the feeling that it's all right now to forgive someone else, we may be sitting there a long, long time. Often, you have to decide to forgive even when your feelings don't want to; it's an act of the will that frees you from carrying around that burden of hurt or shame. As long as you can't forgive someone else or yourself, you are immobilized, and will continue to be plagued by anger or guilt, until you begin to forgive. Forgiveness is a process. It takes time. It may take years to completely forgive someone for the hurt they did to you. But you have to start somewhere. At first, forgiveness changes us, rather than the other person. We are freed up from that burden of anger and hurt. The other person may eventually change or may not. You can't control what they do.

I included forgiving yourself along with forgiving someone else because the internalized guilt you may feel from something you've done in the past is just as oppressive as the anger you feel towards someone else who hurt you. That's why Jesus wanted us to know that we were forgiven. In the Lord's Prayer, Jesus told us to repeat, "Forgive us our sins, as we forgive others." Forgiveness frees us up to be unburdened children of God. That's why Jesus told the story about the Prodigal Son and forgave the woman taken in adultery, so that we would know to seek forgiveness out for ourselves. If He forgives us, why shouldn't we be able to forgive ourselves? And once we have experienced the relief of receiving God's forgiveness, why shouldn't we, as God's people, extend God's forgiveness to those who have hurt us, just like the Prodigal's father did to his son, or as Hosea did to Gomer?

STUDY QUESTIONS

1. When you were a teenager, what did you think life would be like when you left home?

2. Which of the characters in Jesus' story of the Prodigal Son do you identify with the most?

3. What might you want to tell a newly married couple about the importance of forgiveness?

4. Put yourself in the place of the married couple Hosea and Gomer. How do you imagine Hosea felt to forgive Gomer for breaking their marriage bond? How do you imagine Gomer felt being forgiven for breaking their marriage bond?

5. What are some of the intentional or unintentional ways we can hurt each other?

6. What may be some of the day-to-day hurts we need to forgive each other for?

10

St. Paul's Position on Divorce

I Corinthians 7:8-16

In chapter 5, St. Paul's Opinion about Marriage, we read that Paul recommended if people were single, they should stay that way, because life was not easy for Christians if they were active in ministry. That was the main reason he gave for staying single. Life certainly wasn't easy for Paul. While he was in Corinth, he was brought before Gallio, the proconsul, on charges of "persuading people to worship God contrary to the law." But Gallio dismissed the charges. According to Paul's testimony in 2 Corinthians 11:24-27, his life was full of peril. Five times he received 39 lashes, three times beaten with rods, once stoned, three times shipwrecked, floating for a night and day on open sea, constantly on the move, always in danger, hungry, thirsty, cold and naked. Paul's life as an itinerant evangelist did not allow putting down roots, working 9 to 5, and sharing a stable life with wife and family. But he didn't demand such singleness of everybody. If you weren't gifted for singleness, Paul said go ahead and get married, particularly if your sex drives were strong. Go ahead and get married if you can't control yourself and are burning with passion for another. He's being very realistic and pragmatic. Passion is part of a Christian's life, not just a non-Christian's, and sex is part of a Christian marriage, just as it is of a non-Christian's marriage.

Look at what Paul says about divorce in I Corinthians 7:8-16.

> 8 *"But I say to the unmarried and to widows, it is good for them if they remain even as I am.* 9 *But if they don't have self-control, let them marry. For it's better to marry than to burn.* 10 *But to the married I command— not I, but the Lord—that the wife not leave her husband* 11 *(but if she departs, let her remain unmarried, or else be reconciled to her husband), and that the husband not leave his wife.*
>
> 12 *But to the rest I—not the Lord—say, if any brother has an unbelieving wife, and she is content to live with him, let him not leave her.* 13 *The woman who has an unbelieving husband, and he is content to live with her, let her not leave her husband.* 14 *For the unbelieving husband is sanctified in the wife, and the unbelieving wife is sanctified in the husband. Otherwise your children would be unclean, but now they are holy.* 15 *Yet if the unbeliever departs, let there be separation. The brother or the sister is not under bondage in such cases, but God has called us in peace.* 16 *For how do you know, wife, whether you will save your husband? Or how do you know, husband, whether you will save your wife?"* (I Corinthians 7:8-16)

As Paul started out chapter 7, he was replying to some Christian leaders in the Corinthian church who were teaching that getting married would corrupt you, and if you were married, you should get divorced to get free of the corrupting power of sex. Paul turned that around and said that there are situations where not getting married would be even more corrupting. Temptations were all around Corinth, filled with sailors and traders and the temple of Aphrodite, the goddess of love, and only a few had God's gift to remain single without temptation. For the rest, it was better to get married, so their passions had an outlet that was healthy and holy. Furthermore, he went on, when a person became a Christian, but their spouse was not a believer, it was not a reason to get divorced. That's what some of the Corinthians were actually instructing new Christians: when you become a believer in Jesus Christ, your desire should be to be so close to God and serving Him to the fullest, that you should get divorced so you can devote yourselves to your new faith. Sex is a distraction, and in their minds, corrupting and unclean. I find it amazing how people over the centuries have often portrayed the Bible and the Apostle Paul as seeing sex as bad. It wasn't Paul — it was the ascetic Christians in Corinth who portrayed sex as bad.

The Corinthian ideas about marriage were all wrong. If passionate married couples were to divorce to become singles in a drive to be holy, it would violate the Lord's will, not just Paul's. Paul says in verses 10 and 11 that staying married is a command from the Lord, not just his. Elsewhere in this chapter Paul is very clear about what is his opinion and not the Lord's command. In verse 6 he says: "I say this by concession, not as a command." And in verse 12, Paul admits, "I say this, not the Lord." In verse 17, he says, "I give this direction in all the churches." In verse 25, he says, "I don't offer any command from the Lord, but I give my opinion as one who is trustworthy." In verse 40, he says "According to my opinion." But verse 10, Paul says, is not just from him. It's a command from the Lord for married Christians, and it goes: "A wife shouldn't divorce her husband." At the end of the verse he says the same goes for husbands, "A husband shouldn't divorce his wife." In response to the wrong-headed teaching in the Corinth church that new Christians should divorce their spouses, Paul's reaction is "absolutely not." From the beginning, as far back as Genesis 2:24, God intended for our marriages to last forever. Remind yourself what God said marriage was supposed to be by reading Genesis 2:24 again.

> ²⁴ *"Therefore a man will leave his father and his mother, and will join with his wife, and they will be one flesh." (Genesis 2:24)*

Note that the command "not to divorce" in I Corinthians 7:10-11 of applies to both husband and wife, just like the rest of Paul's teachings in this chapter. This command is not like Jewish law, where only a husband could divorce a wife, and for almost any reason. This is a law for Christian couples that comes straight from Jesus. In Mark 10, Jesus says that from our creation, God intended men and women to be united into one flesh, and never be separated. He explains that divorce was only permitted in the law of Moses because of our sin.

For people who have become members of the Kingdom of God through faith in Jesus Christ as Lord and Savior, there should be no need for divorce. That's because if we both believe in Jesus, and if we both have submitted our lives to him, He has become part of our marriage. We're not in it alone. Issues that come up in our marriage aren't something we decide unilaterally, as if just one person made the decision to get married and that same person is free to decide when to get out. The marriage covenant we signed when we wrote our names on the license at the end of the ceremony was not just between us—God was there too. If there are problems, God should be included in the search for solutions. Whatever struggle we're in, health problems, job searches or finances, the challenges of raising kids in a blended family, or conflicts over who's in charge, God wants us to work it through together as a three-some. We should rely on the strong conviction that God has brought us together for a reason. And that reason might well be to work through precisely this time of trouble together, so that we might grow through the pain and come out the other side with our faith strengthened along with our marriage.

But Paul immediately goes on in this passage to give an exception to this command not to divorce. Even though Paul just got through saying Christians should not get divorced, he states an exception in verse 11. There's no reason given in this verse for the wife separating from or divorcing her husband, but if she does, Paul says she should either remain unmarried or be reconciled to her husband. That's because this command not to divorce is for couples where both are followers of Jesus Christ, and he expects them to understand Jesus' teaching that marriage in the Kingdom of God is something that lasts forever.

This command "not to divorce" also applies to Christians in a marriage where the other spouse is not a believer but wants to stay in the marriage. We see this in verses 12 and 13. "The rest" Paul addresses in verse 12 are couples where one spouse is a believer and the other is not. In this case, Paul says if you are the believer, and your non-believing spouse decides to stay with you in spite of your becoming a believer, you are not to divorce them. Paul says this to both men and women believers in Corinth, who are being erroneously told by some in the church, that now that they have become Christians, they should divorce their unbelieving spouses so they aren't tainted by their unbelief. Paul again says, "Absolutely not!"

Look at verse 14. Being a Christian sanctifies your marriage, even if your spouse isn't a believer. If you are a Christian, it should make a difference in your family in the decisions that are made — about your money, how you raise your children, how you treat your neighbors — even if your spouse isn't a believer. Furthermore, if you are a believer, your faith can affect your unbelieving partner. In verse 16, Paul says, "How do you know if you can save your spouse?" and I think he meant, "Through your faith, your spouse might come to salvation. You shouldn't write them off." But Paul gives another exception in verse 15. If the unbelieving spouse leaves, let them go. If you are a Christian married to an unbeliever, and they want to divorce you because of your faith, Paul says to let them go. Paul says you are not bound in such circumstances. In other words, the bonds of marriage are broken, and you are free. In the language of this chapter, "being unbound" means free to remarry, as we'll see later on when we study verse 27.

I want you to notice that Paul doesn't cover every possible situation concerning marriage. He was speaking to situations current in the church at Corinth. He doesn't get as specific about sex, marriage, and divorce in any other letter. So, Paul doesn't say anything about cases like: You are a Christian, you think your spouse is a Christian, but they divorce you. Nor does he explain what other exceptions might be valid reasons for divorcing your spouse, such as abuse or infidelity, although Jesus discussed that in Matthew 5:32. If our marriages become troubled, we need to spend time in prayer and study of scripture, and consulting with other Christians. Then we need to trust in God's compassion and forgiveness. Just like with other things we do that are displeasing to God, even in the mistakes we may have made that led to a failed marriage, if we ask God for forgiveness, He grants it and restores us to himself. 1 John 1:9 says, "But if we confess our sins, he is faithful and righteous to forgive us our sins and cleanse us from all unrighteousness." You'll hear no "Yes, buts" from God. If we are forgiven, we are forgiven, and there should be no doubts about it.

Study Questions

1. What do you think might be different about a Christian marriage compared to that of a non-Christian couple?

2. What are some of the reasons marriages fail, even among Christians?

3. What tools do you think Christians might have at their disposal to help resolve conflicts in their marriages that non-Christians might not be aware of?

4. If you had a son or daughter who married someone who was not a Christian, what advice might you give them about their marriage?

11

JESUS' POSITION ON DIVORCE

MATTHEW 5:31-32 AND 19:3-10

In the Sermon on the Mount, Jesus devotes almost all of chapter 5 to relationships between people. Right after his discussion of anger in Matthew 5:21-26, and adultery in verses 27-30, Jesus talks about divorce in verses 31 and 32.

> *31 "It was also said, 'Whoever shall put away his wife, let him give her a writing of divorce,' 32 but I tell you that whoever puts away his wife, except for the cause of sexual immorality, makes her an adulteress; and whoever marries her when she is put away commits adultery." (Matthew 5:31-32)*

Divorce is another side to the love issue, which many of us have been through. We know how fragile a marriage can be, and how much work it takes to make it succeed. We also know that love is not romance and infatuation, but instead giving yourself to another person during both the good times and the bad. True love involves a combined effort of the heart and mind, of commitment and willpower, not just the product of glands and emotions. Divorce occurs when such true love is no longer there to bind the couple together. But, in his statements on divorce, Jesus is actually telling us something about marriage that we need to hear and take to heart.

Basically, Jesus is saying here, and in his other sayings on divorce and remarriage, that God intended marriage to be forever. When I study the Bible, I always try to uphold three basic rules of interpretation, so that I will arrive at the correct understanding of what God wants me to apply to my life. The first is called "eisegesis vs. exegesis." Simply stated, that means I need to let scripture have authority over me, rather than me over scripture. I need to listen to what God's word says to me and my situation, rather than searching eagerly for some verse that will defend what I want to do. That's particularly important when we come to the subject of divorce and remarriage, because the temptation is to twist verses to say what I want, rather than obeying what they say. But, that doesn't relieve me of the responsibility of trying to understand what difficult passages, like this one, really meant.

So the second principle is that scriptures need to be understood in their context, not just a few words lifted out of the Bible by themselves. How would Jesus' listeners have understood his words? What was the historical and social background he was addressing at that moment? And, because Jesus is the Messiah bringing God's Kingdom to Earth, how does that affect the meaning of his words? Once I understand those background issues, then I can better determine their meaning for today. The third principle is to let scripture help interpret scripture. We shouldn't take one verse in isolation from the rest of the Bible and let it be our sole guiding principle in life, for several reasons: 1) any important topic takes more than one brief sentence to understand and apply it; and, 2) Jesus talked about important issues more than once, and so did Paul and the other apostles. So to get the complete picture, we need to look at the rest of the Bible. For example, let's read Matthew 19:3-10 to see another situation where Jesus taught on the subject of divorce and remarriage. We need to keep in mind as we read this section that Jesus was engaged in a rabbinic debate with other Rabbis, and so the flow of his logic follows rabbinic style, making it harder for us to understand in the 21st century.

> *3 "Pharisees came to him, testing him, and saying, "Is it lawful for a man to divorce his wife for any reason?"*

> *4 He answered, "Haven't you read that he who made them from the beginning made them male and female, 5 and said, 'For this cause a man shall leave his father and mother, and shall be joined to his wife; and the two shall become one flesh?' 6 So that they are no more two, but one flesh. What therefore God has joined together, don't let man tear apart."*

> *7 They asked him, "Why then did Moses command us to give her a certificate of divorce, and divorce her?"*

> *8 He said to them, "Moses, because of the hardness of your hearts, allowed you to divorce your wives, but from the beginning it has not been so. 9 I tell you that whoever divorces his wife, except for sexual immorality, and marries another, commits adultery; and he who marries her when she is divorced commits adultery."*

> *10 His disciples said to him, "If this is the case of the man with his wife, it is not expedient to marry." (Matthew 19:3-10)*

The disciples lived in a time and culture when divorce was easy for a husband to obtain, and virtually impossible for wives to obtain. There was a lot of argument going on in the first century between various rabbinical schools over what was a legitimate reason for divorce. There was no question about whether divorce was legal if the husband initiated it — that was allowed in Deuteronomy 24:1-2.

> *¹ "When a man takes a wife and marries her, then it shall be, if she finds no favor in his eyes, because he has found some unseemly thing in her, that he shall write her a certificate of divorce, and put it in her hand, and send her out of his house. ² When she has departed out of his house, she may go and be another man's wife." (Deuteronomy 24:1-2)*

This passage says that a husband was allowed to divorce his wife if she was displeasing due to something unseemly or indecent in her. But Moses never spelled out what unseemly, displeasing, or indecent meant. So the Rabbis tried to clarify that verse. Rabbi Shammai said that the only acceptable reason for divorce was adultery, and on that the law was clear. Both parties to the adultery were to be taken out and stoned to death. But Rabbi Hillel taught that a man could divorce his wife for almost any reason at all, just as the Pharisees asked Jesus in verse 3, when they tried to embroil him in the scholarly debate over divorce. Rabbi Hillel's disciples taught that a man could divorce his wife for such reasons as: she was not as beautiful in the morning as she had been the night before; or, she burned his breakfast; or, he saw another woman more beautiful. Rabbi Hillel's opinions prevailed, so all a man had to do was write out on a piece of paper, "I divorce you," and give it to his wife, and that was the end of the marriage.

Deuteronomy 24:2 says that after the divorce both the husband and wife would be free to marry again. The former marriage was over, as if it had never happened. The man could remarry because it was obvious that his former wife was unsuited to him in some way, and he needed a wife more suitable. The divorced woman had the certificate of divorce, which was a permission slip for her to remarry, because there wasn't much room in Jewish society for unmarried women, unless they turned to prostitution to survive.

I want you to notice that in Matthew 19:4, Jesus moved the focus from the reasons for divorce to the basis for marriage. Jesus referred back to Genesis 2:24 and creation where God's intent was for man and woman to be united and become one. Here we find the words that are so often used in marriage ceremonies, "What God has joined together, let no man put asunder." God intended us to get married and live happily ever after. He did not intend for marriages to breakdown, and for people who were united into one flesh, to split apart into two again. He knew that memories and unresolved angers would stick with us long after a marriage dissolved. In Matthew 19:8, Jesus tells us that it was only because of people's hard hearts that Moses allowed for divorce. The phrase "hard hearts" brings to mind people who don't care about each other, people whom God can't get through to, people who aren't willing to learn, and grow, and change as marriage requires.

But divorce was not what God intended from the beginning, as Jesus says in verse 8. Then he gives his disciples examples of what he meant about marriage being forever, and in doing so, he says some things in stark contrast with the Jewish law. Jesus said in verse 9 that if a man divorces his wife, and marries another woman, he commits adultery against her. That's a statement of equal treatment that was unheard of in the first century. Verse 9 is similar to chapter 5, verse 32, which assigns the adultery to the woman's side.

From a first century Jewish mindset, neither of Jesus' statements about divorce makes sense, because if a man divorced his wife, the marriage was over, and marrying another would not be adulterous at all for either party — unless one thing had happened: he had neglected to give her a bill of divorce. In Matthew 5:32, Jesus makes it clear that a wife's adultery was legitimate grounds for putting away one's wife. But the result should have been stoning, just as the woman caught in adultery in John 8:4 was brought to Jesus for final judgment. If the "putting away" was for any other reason, and he did not provide her with a bill of divorce, then he was making it appear that she had been immoral. Without a bill of divorce in hand, she was not totally clear and free of her first marriage, and she bore the stigma of having being sent away under an aura of shame. If she married again, she would be committing adultery because she didn't have clear title, so to speak, and the man she married would also be an adulterer, because she was still another man's wife. Jesus makes it clear that the situation is not her fault when he says that the man who sent her away "makes her to be an adulteress" — she didn't do it; he did. Jesus' sympathy was with the woman's predicament, and the injustice inflicted on her by her first husband. Ultimately, Jesus was looking for a change in mindset, to go beyond the Law of Moses, and the arguments of the Rabbis, and focus on what God intended for marriage. In God's perfect world, a marriage would last forever, which becomes our goal as followers of Jesus in God's Kingdom.

Some people, and I think frequently it's those who have never been through a divorce, remind us that in many translations of Malachi 2:16, God says that He hates divorce. No one hates divorce more than someone who has been through it! Divorce is destructive, and no one would seek it out if they didn't feel it was necessary. But people often forget that God himself went through a divorce. Jeremiah 3:8 reports God saying, "I gave Israel her divorce papers and sent her away because of her adultery." So yes, God hates divorce because it represents a broken relationship that even He had with His people. But God hating divorce does not mean that divorce does not happen, even if it's not what God intended for marriage. Frankly, for those couples in a strong relationship with God, divorce should not need to be even considered, because resources are available to help resolve conflicts and differences. But if one or both of the couple take their eyes off Jesus, and put the desires of their own self first, then trouble may certainly come.

We live in a world where people are basically the same as they were 2000 years ago, although the laws have changed. Today, there are no legal restrictions on divorce or remarriage or adultery. Marriages still break down, divorces still happen, and so does adultery. Because of sin that husbands commit against wives and wives against husbands, marriage breakdowns are going to happen, and sometimes divorce is the only solution to a difficult situation. Divorce is ugly, it is a misfortune, it is destructive, but divorce itself is not sin. The sins of dishonesty, selfishness, addiction, deception, or abuse are committed in the marriage long before the divorce happens. If we were totally honest, I think we'd all confess that there was sin on both sides that brought about our own divorces. The late George Moore, former Associate Pastor of Adult Education at First Presbyterian Church in Colorado Springs, said more than once, "In a marriage breakdown, there's enough sin to go around." Some sins are overt, like adultery, abuse or addiction. But some sins are less obvious, such as withdrawal, deceit, manipulation, or enabling the other's destructive behavior. But they are all sin, and any sin undermines a relationship.

Jesus' statements on marriage are hard, like many of the things Jesus said. His pronouncement that marriage is forever is like many of Jesus' other pronouncements that we find in the Sermon on the Mount. Things like not being angry with your brother, not resisting someone who takes your cloak, to love your enemies and pray for those who persecute you, not to worry about your source of food or clothing — that God will provide. These are the laws of the Kingdom of God that Jesus taught, rather than the laws of humankind. When the Kingdom of God is fully come, the lion will lie down with the lamb, says Isaiah. When the Kingdom of God is fully come, we will all have the love of God written on our hearts, says Jeremiah. There will be no hunger, no sickness, no death, and no poverty. There will be no lying, no abuse, no cheating, no put-downs, no insults, no arguing, and no fighting. There will be no more sin, no more hate, no more crying, no more broken marriages, no more adultery, and no more divorce.

In Jesus' pronouncements, we find him setting forth the ideals, the models, for us to pattern ourselves against as Christians. If this were a perfect world, if the Kingdom of God were fully come, they would be totally natural for us. But the Kingdom of God is not yet complete. It will only be complete when Jesus comes again. In the meantime, we are both saved, and yet being saved. We are free from sin, and yet still sinners. As the Apostle Paul said, we struggle within because we have an old nature that is subject to the law of sin, but also a new nature that is subject to the law of God.

All the while, we have the mercy of God. We have his forgiveness when we come to him in confession for our sins. I hope you have asked God for forgiveness for what happened in a previous marriage. I hope you asked God for forgiveness for the sins that brought about that break down in a relationship that you expected to last forever. Before I married Pegi, I struggled about what had gone wrong with my former marriage, and whether remarriage was right for me. I had been a Baptist pastor, and had some training in marriage counseling, so I knew what God expected from marriage, and I had failed. Given that theological and psychological background, how could I feel capable and ready for remarriage? After struggling for a while, I threw myself on the mercy of God, told him I was doing the best I could to follow what he wanted me to do, that I knew I had failed at marriage, but I believed He wanted me to marry Pegi, and all I could do was ask for His forgiveness for the past, and His blessings and strength for the future.

Forgiveness is key to understanding Jesus' approach to us. He gives us the ideals, the way life should be if there were no sin; but because sin still exists in this world, he gives us mercy and forgiveness. Remember the woman taken in adultery? Jesus told the men who had come to stone her, "Let him who is without sin cast the first stone," and there was no one there without sin, except Jesus, and he forgave her. Remember Peter denying Jesus three times the night of Jesus' trial, and yet Jesus forgave him and gave him another chance. When asked how many times must we forgive, Jesus told us seventy times seven, and that's the kind of forgiveness he gives to us who have been through the pain and shame of a marriage breakdown and divorce. And like Peter, we too have been given another chance to form the holy and enduring partnership that God intended in marriage.

Study Questions

1. Do you have any idea what Jesus was getting at in the passage we read, when he says, "If a man divorces his wife, he causes her to become an adulteress"?

2. Why do you think the disciples reacted so negatively in Matthew 19:10 about Jesus' position on marriage?

3. How different do you think the significance of divorce in today's society is than in the first century?

4. What does it take to make a marriage last for the rest of a couple's life together?

5. How have you felt God's forgiveness in your marriage or committed relationship?

12

ST. PAUL DISCUSSES REMARRIAGE

I CORINTHIANS 7:25-28

An important principle for interpreting the Bible is understanding the situations that led to the writing, so we don't make mistakes when we apply what we read to our modern situation. When Paul wrote chapter 7, he was dealing with specific issues and questions of the Corinthians. Paul did not write this chapter as a rule book to cover all situations, but to respond to the issues they were dealing with. They wrote to him and asked for his opinions, and Paul wrote back to deal with problems in the church he had heard about, and to answer their questions. Paul gives us clues to when he changes topics in the way he organized his thoughts. For example, chapter 7, verse 1 starts out "Regarding the issues you wrote about," and those issues about which they were confused had to do with marriage. Chapter 8 verse 1 starts out "Regarding food sacrificed to idols," which really is about how a newly converted Christian lives in a pagan society. Chapter 12 verse 1 starts out "Regarding spiritual gifts," which dealt with the proper exercise of spirituality in the congregation. So in chapter 7, Paul was dealing with specific issues concerning marriage and divorce among Corinthian Christians.

The sanctity of marriage is the foundation of Paul's approach to marriage and divorce. When we read verses 25-28 of chapter 7, we need to remember the situation in

Corinth that Paul is addressing, where people were debating how marriage fits into the Christian life, and some have already expressed their opinion that being single was better than being married. In a previous section, we saw how Paul refuted the recommendation of some church leaders in Corinth that married people should get divorced, so they could devote themselves to religion. Now, Read I Corinthians 7:25-28 to see how Paul handles the issue of what to do if you are single.

> 25 *"Now concerning virgins, I have no commandment from the Lord, but I give my judgment as one who has obtained mercy from the Lord to be trustworthy.* 26 *Therefore I think that because of the distress that is on us, that it's good for a man to remain as he is.* 27 *Are you bound to a wife? Don't seek to be freed. Are you free from a wife? Don't seek a wife.* 28 *But if you marry, you have not sinned. If a virgin marries, she has not sinned. Yet such will have oppression in the flesh, and I want to spare you." (I Corinthians 7:25-28)*

Verses 25 and 26 are Paul's opinion about what singles should do. The word translated *virgin* is the Greek word *parthenos*, which usually means unmarried woman, but can also mean unmarried man. Greek doesn't have a separate word for each sex to specifically indicate the unmarried state. I don't think Paul is talking about people who haven't had sex, as much as he is people who aren't married. In other words, singles. His advice — he calls it a judgment and not a command in verse 25 — to the singles in Corinth is to stay as they are, as we see in verse 26. The reason he gives for his advice is "Because of the coming crisis." We don't know exactly what that crisis was. We can presume it was a time of persecution for the new Christians in Corinth. Perhaps someone in Corinth had asked whether it was better for singles to get married or to stay single during this time of persecution, and Paul's response to them was to stay single, as they were. Actually, in verse 29, Paul goes on to say that what he means is that the time is short. And at the end of verse 31 he says that this present world is passing away. If we put two and two together, we might conclude that Paul expected Jesus to return soon to earth, and the crisis in Corinth was a sign of his immanent return. Given that, Christians should be concerned with evangelizing, spreading the good news, not with falling in love and getting married. If this sense of urgency was true for singles, it was also true for married people. This was not a time for big changes in your lifestyle, whether single or married. If you are single, don't get married. If you are married, don't seek a divorce.

But Paul knows that those rules can't be universal. If no singles had ever married from that point on, the human race would have died out. People fall in love even under the most difficult circumstances. I would bet that in the midst of the conflicts, or in disasters such as earthquakes and floods, people are falling in love and getting married. And Paul also knew that staying married was not absolute either. Divorce would happen. Even though he said Christians should not get divorced, he acknowledged there were exceptions, such as a spouse who was not a believer and decides to leave. Matthew's gospel (5:32) also adds the exception of unfaithfulness as a reason for divorce. The church has always struggled over this dilemma. If people are truly being Christian and truly loving their spouses, why should there be any grounds for divorce?

The basic problem we're dealing with is "what is a Christian," and we have to be very careful here. We don't want to go on witch-hunts deciding who is a Christian and who isn't, because we aren't perfect enough ourselves to do that. If being a Christian means living up to everything Jesus taught in the Sermon on the Mount, then not one of us is a Christian. But you don't become a Christian just because your parents were. You can't inherit a gene that makes you Christian. You're not a Christian just because you were baptized, or you come to church and Sunday School, although a Christian will do those things. You're not a Christian just because you teach or preach in that church or Sunday School, either, although Christians teach and preach. You're not a Christian just because you read your Bible and pray, although these spiritual practices are something a Christian will do. You're not a Christian just because you assent to a list of doctrines or a confession published by a church, although Christians do have some common beliefs and values. You're not a Christian just because you raise your hand or come forward at an invitation given at some service or camp, although that's how many people start the Christian life. And you're not a Christian just because you are a good person and do good works, although Christians by and large are good people and do good works. The Apostle Paul was very clear that it's not what you do that makes you right with God, it's your faith and trust in Jesus Christ as Savior and Lord. When we give him that trust, God gives back his grace that gives us the power to live a life of good works. And as the Apostle James tells us, that if we say we have faith, but it isn't matched by good works enabled by God's grace, then it's a dead faith; it's not real.

If a person is abusive to their spouse and family, they are not showing the good works one can legitimately expect to flow from Christian faith. If someone continually has affairs outside of the bonds of marriage, they are defying the intentions of God for the unity of man and woman. If a wife or husband does not trust that God loves them and has brought them into marriage for their own growth and betterment, so that they seek comfort from someone else, they are showing the weakness of unbelief. If anyone allows the insidious power of drugs and alcohol to deprive their family of sustenance and care, they are worshipping at the altar of a god other than God Almighty. If someone like this refuses to repent and change their ways towards the ones they were given to love, they are showing unbelief in the power of Jesus Christ to change them and make them holy. Are there reasons for divorce? As long as there is unfaithfulness, as long as there is sin, there will be divorce, even in what you might have thought was a Christian marriage.

Because of all these reasons, in Corinth there were divorced Christians who would now fit in the category of *parthenos*, or single. What was Paul's advice to them? Look at verses 27 and 28. Verse 27 doesn't say, "If you are married" as some translations have it — it literally says, "if you have been bound to a woman." Bound means tied up. We talk about the bonds of matrimony, and it means the same thing. If you are married, there is figuratively a rope tied between you and your wife, linking you two together. When you get divorced, that rope is untied, you are unbound, you are loosed from your spouse. That's what the Greek word *lusin* literally means, "loosed." It means divorced. So Paul says, "if you are married don't get divorced." But the next sentence starts out with the same word *lusin*, but it's in a past passive tense *lelusai*. It doesn't mean "unmarried" as some translations have it, it means "divorced," just like it did in the previous sentence. Paul is saying to them, "Have you been loosed from a woman, or divorced? If so, don't get married." But he doesn't stop there. He goes on to say, in spite of all the advice he's just given, if you do marry, whether you were single, or whether you were divorced, you do not sin. I think Paul's message is: If you are divorced, and decide to get married again, you are not sinning. And the word "virgin" found in many translations is that Greek word *parthenos* again, which as we showed above can mean unmarried young man as well as unmarried young woman, in other words, someone who is "single." So to the confused Corinthians, Paul says if you are single, whether never married or now divorced, it is OK to go ahead and get married. But he goes on to warn them that it won't necessarily make life easier. Paul says in the rest of verse 28, "But those who marry will face many added struggles, and I am trying to spare you such problems." Married life may, in fact, be harder given the troubled times ahead.

Conclusion:

Based on all this study of what the Bible teaches about Love, Marriage, Divorce and Remarriage, my conclusions are:

1. God's intention for marriage was that it be forever.

2. Marriage is broken by our sin, which happens because we lose faith in God.

3. Divorce is the legal recognition that the marriage is broken. In our American culture, divorce can be initiated by either party, and is difficult to stop once the process has started. It takes two willing partners to make a marriage, not just one.

4. Forgiveness from God is available for any confessed sin for which you are truly repentant and seek to change, even adultery.

5. Remarriage after divorce is possible, and will be blessed by God, given the overall Biblical testimony, but there are a few cautions that should be observed:

a. A person wanting to remarry needs to examine his/ her behavior in the first marriage thoroughly, and take steps to change what they did that contributed in any way to the breakdown of the relationship. It takes a while. Experts recommend two years minimum to get over the feelings of the past, and learn new ways of relating. People who marry very soon after divorce are very likely to have that marriage fail too.

b. The earlier marriage will continue to have an impact on someone who remarries. There's an emotional tie to the past relationship that never quite goes away. It may take several years before the ghosts of the past fade. The feelings about the past relationship may resurface again and again and will likely affect the new relationship adversely.

c. It may take several years to restore the sense of trust in another person, and solidify a commitment to the new marriage. All too often there's a sense that I've survived divorce before, and if this new marriage doesn't work out, I can divorce again. This attitude can doom the new marriage.

d. Two factors that I believe are necessary for a marriage to succeed are 1) a shared faith and trust in God, 2) a commitment to each other that is greater than all other commitments, other than to God. "All other commitments" include children, friends, past relationships, parents, career, job, hobbies, and even church work.

STUDY QUESTIONS

1. During the time you were single after a marriage dissolved or was ended by the death of your spouse, what did you think of the idea of getting married again?

2. If Paul had known that nearly 2000 years later, we'd be looking to him for advice on divorce and remarriage, what might he have said?

3. What can make a marriage between Christian people fall apart?

4. What might be some of the characteristics of a Christian marriage as opposed to a non-Christian marriage?

5. If you have been or are going to be remarried, what have been some of the reactions when you told people you were going to remarry?

6. In I Corinthians 7:28, Paul says he wanted to save them from the troubles of being married.. What troubles do you think he might be referring to?

7. What are some of the most important things a couple can do to keep their marriage strong and healthy?

13

LEARNING TO TRUST

In a remarriage, let alone in a first marriage, one very difficult but extremely important task is to learn to trust another person with yourself. Trust is absolutely critical to a healthy marriage and family. If a person has been through a divorce, trust was broken, and the ability to trust another person needs to be rebuilt. It doesn't come instantaneously, but grows through experience. You reveal something of your inner self, and trust grows if your spouse treats that revelation with respect and confidentiality. Trust in marriage includes the relationship between husband and wife, between children and parents, and particularly between step-children and step-parents. Let's look at what the Bible says about trust. The Old Testament has many verses that encourage us to trust God. Read Psalm 20:7, Psalm 25:1-2 and Proverbs 3:5 to see some representative Old Testament passages about trust, and who we can trust.

7 "Some trust in chariots, and some in horses,
but we trust the name of Yahweh our God." (Psalm 20:7)

1 "To you, Yahweh, do I lift up my soul.
2 My God, I have trusted in you.
   Don't let me be shamed.
   Don't let my enemies triumph over me."
   (Psalm 25:1-2)

5 "Trust in Yahweh with all your heart,
   and don't lean on your own understanding."
   (Proverbs 3:5)

Proverbs 3:5 is that famous passage, "Trust in the Lord with all your heart." There's nothing in the Old Testament that suggests that we can trust our fellow man or woman the same way we can trust God. That's because the Old Testament had a very clear picture of how sin can take hold of the best of people and bring hurt to their lives and the lives of the ones they love. The message is clear, you can trust God implicitly to always love you and do the best for you, but you can't say the same thing about fellow human beings. Some people may find trusting God to be difficult, because they've never seen a good human example of trust. We may have heard about God's unconditional love, but have never truly experienced that kind of love from a human being, so we have trouble believing it can be ours. In the same way, when we trust someone else, it doesn't mean we can expect them to be perfect like God is perfect, because they'll ultimately let us down.

The Greek words used for trust in the New Testament help us better understand what it means to trust someone. One word Paul uses meaning trust is *pepoithos*, which is translated "having confidence" or "being sure" or "persuaded." That kind of trust is like a mountain climber trying a rope to make sure it'll hold. He doesn't climb until he's confident in the rope. That's a *pepoithos* kind of trust. Another Greek word often translated "trust" is *elpidzo,* but it has the base meaning "to hope," which can be quite different than "being sure." Hoping that your spouse will be loyal to you is different than trusting that they will be. A third Greek word, *pistis,* is usually translated "faith" and the related verb *pisteuo* is usually translated "to believe." but both words have a base meaning that is closer to "trust." Paul's famous words in I Corinthians 13:7, *panta pisteuei*, have been translated "Love always trusts" or "Love believes all things." The word *pisteuei* means both to believe and to trust, which sheds some light on the depth of meaning for trusting another. Remember that in John 3:16, we find the same word. "God so loved the world that he gave his only begotten Son, that whosoever believes in Him shall not perish, but have everlasting life." The last part of the verse could also be translated "whoever trusts in Him will not perish." Believing doesn't mean just accepting a list of theological facts about Jesus, like he was born and died on a cross for our sins and was raised from the dead to bring us new life, although that's all true. Believing in Jesus means to trust Him with your life, because God can be trusted.

Psychologists tell us that we learn to trust or not trust the people in our lives at an early age, before the age of two in fact. Think of it! Whether you can trust your parents or spouse or teacher or boss or the police or the preacher, you learn before you are out of diapers. That's because when you are a baby in your crib, you need other people to service your basic needs. If you are hungry, you cry and someone comes and gives you milk or food. If you feel wet, you cry and someone comes and changes you. If you are bored and feel lonely, you cry and someone comes and plays with you. Or they don't come, and you stay hungry or wet or lonely. And you form an opinion in your infant brain about whether you can trust those big people you need so desperately. As you grow up, that early opinion gets reinforced by what happens to you. If you are physically or emotionally abused as a child, your opinion that people can't be trusted becomes more concrete. If you are loved and affirmed, you are more likely to think people can be trusted. Those feelings about trustworthiness of others often are projected onto God, because we often see God as just a bigger and more powerful parent, who's supposed to do everything right for us. So now, let's imagine that we've grown up, we've married, settled down, gotten established in our jobs, had a few kids—and then the bottom falls out, and we find ourselves divorced. Or maybe our spouse dies and leaves us alone with the kids to raise, and debts to pay. Often, people find themselves hooked back into their childhood fears that people can't be trusted.

Becoming a Christian helps you learn how to trust other people, because you learn that you can trust God. As you grow in faith you experience the Holy Spirit working in your life to help you become trustworthy. It takes two people to make a healthy marriage: on one side you have to learn to trust, and on the other, you have to learn how to be trustworthy. While loving someone else is a decision you make rather than something that's earned, trust, on the other hand, *is* something that's earned, based on experience. In other words, to be considered trust-worthy, you have to show yourself to be dependable, like the mountain climber's rope. But to be trusting, you have to learn first to test the rope, and then to climb it. One of the tasks of the first year of marriage is learning you can trust your spouse in different situations.

Another issue with trust involves our children and step-children. When we go through a divorce, they are just as affected by it as we are, although they may not be able to voice their worries or anger the same way we can. Their trust in their parents and the goodness of life has been shattered. They don't know what's going on, or what part they played in this tragedy, and for some of them, all they know is that the two people they loved and trusted most are now at odds with each other, and, as children, they are right smack in the middle of it all.

When St. Paul wrote to new Christians in Corinth or Colossae, for example, he was talking to people who had come out of paganism into faith in Jesus. They needed to put away some behaviors that were common in their culture, and put on some new ways of living. As Christians, they had a chance to start over and live lives pleasing to God and considerate and helpful to their spouses and children. Perhaps when Paul told husbands to love their wives it was because in their pagan surroundings, wives were not loved. Perhaps when he told fathers to not provoke their children, it was because children were treated roughly in their pagan environment. Learning to trust another person, and to be trustworthy yourself, is enabled when you let the Holy Spirit come into your heart and mind. The Spirit can help heal your past pain and suspicions and make your heart new. Let the Spirit guide you away from self-centered ways of living and into loving, considerate and dependable ways. That's the kind of love God gives us, and as we learn to let his love change us, we become more like him, so that we can be trustworthy, too.

STUDY QUESTIONS

1. Which of the following ingredients of a healthy marriage — commitment, trust, forgiveness, and hope — do you think might be the most challenging?

2. What would you say it means to trust someone?

3. How have you seen God to be trustworthy in your life?

4. During a courtship, how did you deal with any concerns about being able to trust the other person?

5. What can we do to help our spouses learn to trust us?

6. If you've been a step-parent, what are some things you've learned to help your step-children learn to trust you?

14

THE NECESSITY FOR COMMITMENT

Another extremely important yet difficult requirement for forming a marriage that will last is commitment to each other. Many of us have seen what happens when commitment isn't in a marriage or has broken down. A marriage without commitment eventually dissolves. Let's look more deeply into what that commitment really means. My unabridged dictionary provides a first definition for commitment as "the act of committing," and the second definition as "the state of being committed." Neither of those are helpful. Skipping over those primary definitions to the next group of definitions, it goes on to further define commitment as consignment, as to prison, a mental institution, or a hospital. Now, if I were a comedian, that definition would have a lot of use. I could equate marriage to imprisonment or a locked ward, and get a lot of laughs, because some people find marriage confining, not freeing. But that's not what I was looking for as a way of defining commitment, so I went on. Definition #10 reads, "commitment is a pledge or promise: an obligation." That's more like it, but it still lacked something. After all, in today's world, promises are given lightly, without much thought to how they will be carried out, or in fact whether they will actually be carried out. The word obligation has more to it, but it sounds like something forced on a person, rather than something voluntarily undertaken. So, my own definition for commitment reads like this: "a voluntary pledge by a person to carry out a promise, agreement, or task without fail, as long as they are physically and mentally able to, and to put that activity as a top priority in their lives."

During wedding ceremonies, vows are made between the bride and groom. Here are some traditional vows that couples repeat to each other during wedding ceremonies: "I take you to be my wife (or husband), and I do promise and commit, before God and these witnesses, to be your loving and faithful husband (or wife), and best friend, in plenty and in want, in joy and in sorrow, in sickness and in health, as long as we both shall live." Now, what few people realize is that those vows are the clauses in a legal contract. What do you need for a contract to be legal? 1) A statement of what each party will do — those are the vows. 2) An exchange of something of value, or an acknowledgment of payment for services rendered — the rings, and 3) witnesses. So there you are — your wedding service becomes a legal and binding contract. But how many people treat their vows as if they are somehow obligated to carry them out? "In plenty and in want, in joy and in sorrow, in sickness and in health, as long as we both shall live." That covers most of the situations that will come up in a marriage: job loss, grief, illness, and duration.

Commitment is different than love, because love is the activity of doing something for someone else because they need it. Commitment has to do with keeping your promise to be there with the other, and for the other, and not to take off when the going gets rough. The Bible uses the word "commit" frequently, 43 times according to one concordance. In 18 of those times the word "commit" is used in the phrase "do not commit adultery," or something similar. Adultery is the exchange of intimacy with someone other than the one we have promised to love and cherish forever. Adultery doesn't have to include sex to be adultery, as far as the Bible is concerned. It has to do with forming a close bond with someone other than the one to whom you've been joined. For example, the people of Israel were accused of adultery when they worshipped another god. They broke their commitment to love, honor, and worship the God who led them out of slavery, after He promised to be their God and be in relationship with them forever. The prophets reminded them that commitment to God could not be shared with another object of worship. Read I Samuel 7:3-4 to see the totality of commitment God expected from the people of Israel.

> 3 *"Samuel spoke to all the house of Israel, saying, "If you are returning to Yahweh with all your heart, then put away the foreign gods and the Ashtaroth from among you, and direct your hearts to Yahweh, and serve him only; and he will deliver you out of the hand of the Philistines." 4 Then the children of Israel removed the Baals and the Ashtaroth, and served Yahweh only." (I Samuel 7:3-4)*

Here's a case where the Israelites had set up idols and worshipped them, and had suffered greatly under the domination of the Philistines. The prophet Samuel told them to get rid of those idols and commit themselves to the Lord and serve him only. Then the Lord would deliver them from the Philistine oppression.

From this we learn that commitment requires the turning away of one's allegiance from *any* distraction to following God's way. Our commitment to God and our commitment to our spouse are inseparably linked. We cannot claim to be following God's will if we put aside the commitment to our spouse and find intimacy with someone else, or become pre-occupied with some other activity, no matter how good it may seem.

Remembering that God gave us our spouse to complete us, a helper that fits us as Genesis 2:18 declares, helps us keep both commitments, first to God and then to our spouse. And then the Bible says we will be blessed.

Study Questions

1. How might you extend the author's definition of commitment to marriage? (Commitment is a voluntary pledge by a person to carry out a promise, agreement, or task without fail, as long as they are physically and mentally able to, and to put that activity as a top priority in their lives.)

2. How do you think "love" relates to the commitment to honor your wedding vows? (Traditional vows include: In plenty and in want, in joy and in sorrow, in sickness and in health, as long as we both shall live.)

3. What might challenge a life-long commitment in marriage these days?

4. What are some ways we can let our spouse know we are committed to stay in our marriage even through the struggles that may lie ahead of us?

AFTERWORD

I hope and pray this study into what the Bible says about Love, Marriage, Divorce, and Remarriage has been helpful, comforting, challenging, and hopeful. What we must never forget is that marriage is God's invention. Our spouse is God's child just as much as we are, and He had a purpose in bringing us together. While marriage brings us companionship and comfort, it also gives us many opportunities to work together as a team to accomplish God's will on Earth, become the people God intended us to be, and be honest witnesses and humble examples of what a Christian marriage can be.

Raymond E. Parry